• Bartholomew

WALKING IN THE
LOIRE VALLEY

by Brian Spencer

Bartholomew

An Imprint of HarperCollins*Publishers*

CONTENTS

A Bartholomew Walk Guide
Published by Bartholomew
An Imprint of HarperCollins*Publishers*
77-85 Fulham Palace Road
London W6 8JB

First published 1996
© Bartholomew 1996

Printed in Hong Kong

ISBN 0 7028 3133 6
96/1/15

LOCATION MAP

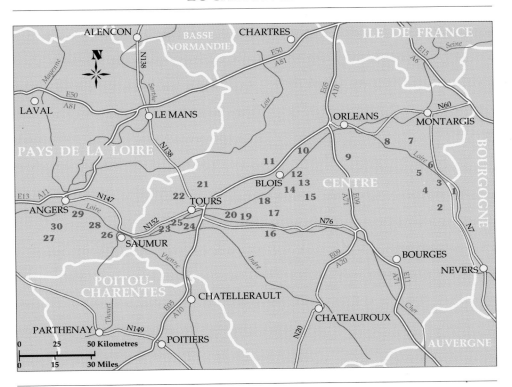

KEY TO ROUTE MAPS

Major Road		Railway/Station		—100—	Contour (metres)
Minor Road		Stream/River		Earthworks	
Track		Built-up area/Building		Cave	
Walk Route		Woodland		† Church or Chapel	
Alternative Route		Orchard		† Calvary or Cross	
Other Footpath		Scrub		Ŧ Picnic Site	
1 Route Description		Vineyard		▲ Camping	
A Point of Interest		Gravel Pit		Viewpoint	
				P Parking	

INTRODUCTION

THE LOIRE

The Loire flows for over 650 miles through many different landscapes. From its source beneath the beehive-shaped Gerbier de Jonc mountain in the Auvergne, to St. Nazaire on the Atlantic Coast, it is the longest river in France. The region is known as the 'Garden of France' because it has a rich alluvial soil and a climate that is never too hot or too cold. Spring starts in late February; a profusion of wild flowers come out and spring vegetables are ready much earlier than in southern England, as they are protected from late frosts by the the mildness of Atlantic breezes. It is probably the climate that makes the people so friendly. They speak the purest French, and they are easy to get on with and welcome visitors.

This guide is devoted to walks around the best known part of the Loire Valley. It is to the central section of the river's lowland course that most visitors have come ever since the Romans conquered the local Celtic tribes. The region was fought over by the English and French until Joan of Arc galvanised the weak Dauphin into action, and the English were finally driven out of the Loire in one of the few decisive actions of the Hundred Years War.

Its strategic importance made the Loire Valley an obvious location for the headquarters of successive French kings. The châteaux, which have become synonymous with the Loire, started to spring up along its banks and in near-by forests in the 10th century. In each phase of château building, architectural styles developed according to the needs of the time. Designs altered in response to the technology of warfare, from the simple arrow-slit defences of Angers and Chinon between 900 and 1200, to more sophisticated defences in the 15th century to combat the increasing use of gunpowder and cannon fire. Chaumont, Saumur and Gien date from this time. In the 16th century, a more peaceful age heralded a flowering of the aesthetics of château design. During this time, the extravagant châteaux of Amboise, Blois, Chambord, Chenonceaux and Villandry were built. Gardens were stylized and formal, such as the complex knot garden at Villandry. In the 17th and 18th centuries château design was less fanciful; stately homes such as Beauregard, Cheverny and Ménars were set in attractive rolling parkland.

The French Revolution brought an end to château building and many were destroyed in the excesses of the 'Terror' which followed. Most of the remaining châteaux that open to the public are under state control and their future is secure. However, there are still those, such as the Château de la Ferté St. Aubin, that rely on semi-voluntary organisations for their upkeep.

Towns and cities began to spring up along the river banks in medieval times, many built on Roman foundations. Modern housing and industrial estates now surround their medieval hearts, but in most town centres the narrow old streets are traffic-free and remain havens of tranquillity. The town centres of Angers and Tours, for example, are lined with tall half-timbered merchants' houses and ancient churches. Christianity came early to the Loire Valley. In St. Benoît-sur-Loire, the tomb of St. Benedict, the patron saint of Europe, is still visited by pilgrims. The soaring abbey churches of Tours and Angers and the famous Rose Windows of Chartres Cathedral continue to instil a sense of awe in their visitors.

Using the Loire as its main artery, commercial traffic plied the river until railways and modern roads overtook this more leisurely means of transport. Canals dug to by-pass shallows were linked to a national network, and it is still possible to cruise from northern France via Paris to the Mediterranean.

WINE AND FOOD

Bearing in mind the Loire's great length, it is not surprising that there are in the region of 60 different *appellations* between its source in the Auvergne to the estuary beyond Nantes. Loire wines are probably France's most versatile and are suitable for almost any occasion. The choice of red, white or rosé, still or sparkling, dry or sweet, means that all tastes and budgets can be satisfied. Probably the best known Loire wines are the Muscadets from Sevre et Main south of Nantes, where those labelled 'Sur Lie' are the better *cuvées*. Anjou wines are grown in the countryside around Angers and Saumur, and further upstream Vouvray is best known for its excellent sparkling wines. The smaller scale wine producing districts of Pouilly and Sancerre, which cover just a few hundred hectares in total, are visited on a number of walks in this guide. Look out for the *dégustation* signs which indicate the locality of merchants or producers inviting you to taste their vintages.

Food in the Loire is simple, but of good quality. Although more likely to be farmed than wild, Loire salmon is invariably on the menu. Eels (*anguilles*) are also popular, either braised in red wine or fried in breadcrumbs with other small river fish in a *friture de la Loire*. Rabbit and pork are commonly offered, or if you prefer a gamier meat, you can eat wild boar (*sanglier*) or jugged hare (*civet de lièvre de Sologne*). Locally grown asparagus is excellent, but make sure it is fresh if you are self-catering. As the Loire Valley is a fruit growing region, fresh cherries, apples, pears and desert grapes can be quite cheap. Goats' cheese (*fromage de chèvre*) is more widely available than cows' cheese. It is sold in a wide range of shapes and colours, from the dark, blue-skinned nutty *Romorantin* to the *Crémets*, which are eaten as a dessert with sugar and cream.

FETES, FESTIVALS AND MAJOR EVENTS

Even the smallest villages celebrate their own saint's day, when everyone turns out in their Sunday 'best' to walk in procession behind a highly decorated statue of their saint or the Virgin Mary.

Larger towns often host events on a grand scale, including some of international importance. The following is a selection of events in towns near walks described in this guide. It is worth making inquiries with local tourist offices to get up-to-date informatin about what is going on.

Amboise
Easter and 15 August – Wine fair.

Angers
End June to mid-July – Anjou festival of concerts, plays, ballet and exhibitions.

Blois
Mid-June – *Floréal Blésois* (carnival, regatta, drama and music).

Bourges
May – *La Veille Ville en Fête* (carnival).
May to October – Audio-visual show, *La Cathédrale de Bourges et les Monuments du Cher*.

Bourgueil
First Saturday in February – Wine fair.

Châteauneuf-sur-Loire
Whitsun – Rhododendron festival.

Cheverny
Mid-July to mid-August – Torchlight meet of hounds, and horn concerts by Trompes de Cheverny.

Chinon
First weekend in August – Medieval market with entertainment by jugglers and dancers, etc.

Doué-la-Fontaine
Mid-July – *Floralies de la Rose* (International Rose Festival).

Gien
Mid-July every odd numbered year – Historical festival, drama and costumed parades.

Jargeau
Mid-October – *Foire des Châtaignes* (chestnut fair).

Langeais
Late July and early August – International music festival at Domaine de Vernou.

Meung-sur-Loire
June and September – Organ concerts at Collégiale St. Liphard.

Montoire-sur-le-Loir
Mid-August – World Folklore Festival (street processions and concerts).

Olivet
Second week in June – Watersports festival on the River Loiret.

Orléans
7 and 8 May – Joan of Arc Festival. Illumination of cathederal on 7 May; religious and secular ceremonies on 8 May.
May to October – Open-air floral displays in Parc Floral de la Source.

Sablé-sur-Sarthe
Last Sunday in May – *Fête du Quéniau* (costumed children's festival).

St. Benoît
Easter Saturday – Vigil and Gregorian chant at the abbey.
Christmas Eve – Gregorian chant at the abbey.

Saumur
Second fortnight in July – *Grand Carrousel* (cavalry display and military tattoo).
Mid-September – Equestrian fortnight.
Sully-sur-Loire
Whitsun week – Orchestral concerts at the château.
Friday and Saturday evenings in July – Music and drama festival at the château.
Last Sunday in October – meet of hounds and concert of hunting horns at the château.
Tours
Last weekend in June and first weekend in July – Touraine music festival at the Grange de Meslay, with international celebrities.
Last fortnight in July – Drama festival.
Early August – Ballet festival in the garden of the Musée des Beaux-Arts.

Châteaux with *Son-et-Lumières*
Amboise
Azay-le-Rideau
Blois
Chambord
Chedigny
Chenonceaux
Loches
Valençay

HOW TO GET TO THE LOIRE

The most direct route from England is by the Brittany Ferries service from Portsmouth to St. Malo, then the the N137 to Rennes. From there take any of the smaller roads south-east, depending on which part of the Loire is your final destination. Alternatively P&O or Sealink ferries from Portsmouth to Cherbourg will link with the N13 to Caen, then the N158 to Alençon. From there the N138 goes direct to Tours via le Mans. Anyone crossing the channel either by the tunnel or ferry can avoid Paris on the way south by using the N1 and A28 from the channel ports to Rouen and then the N138 to the Loire Valley around Tours.

TRAVEL IN FRANCE

Motor insurance
Green Card certificates are no longer required for motoring in France and other member states of the EC. However, you must have an up-to-date insurance policy and have advised your insurer of your plans. Your insurer, either through their broker or agent, will need to know your proposed travel dates and all the countries you intend visiting. Failure to notify your insurer could result in your policy being restricted to the minimum requirements needed to comply with the laws relating to compulsory insurance in any member country of the EC in which the vehicle is being used. Although travel documents are rarely examined on entry to member countries of the EC, it is advisable to carry your motor insurance certificate and the vehicle log book at all times. Your insurance company will advise you about what to do in the event of an accident.

Holders of UK provisional licences are not allowed to drive in France and the minimum age for drivers is 18.

Motoring organisations offer extra insurance which can cover personal accident and medical costs, holiday cancellation and loss of personal property, as well as vehicle breakdown, accident and theft. Their insurance schemes usually cover the cost of a replacement vehicle or the fare to return home, either for the driver and passengers or the vehicle, should the need arise for it to be despatched separately. Most foreign travel insurance schemes offered by the motoring organisations include Letters of Credit which are repayable on return to the UK.

Driving in France
Despite the need to concentrate on driving on the 'wrong' side of the road, motoring in France is often more pleasurable than at home. Roads away from the larger towns are relatively traffic free outside the main holiday periods. However, there are a few simple rules which must be observed when driving in France:
1. Have your motoring documents available at all times.
2. Carry a spare set of bulbs, including indicator bulbs. Failure to do so could result in an on-the-spot fine in the event of a bulb not working.
3. Carry a red warning triangle, and in the event of a break-down or accident, erect it 30 metres (33 yards) behind your car. It must be in clear view without obstructing oncoming traffic.
4. Wearing seat belts is compulsory for all front seat passengers and drivers. Children below ten years are not allowed to travel in the front seat.

5. 'GB' stickers must be as close as possible to the rear number plate.

6. Drink-driving laws are strictly interpreted and arrest for this offence could result in a prison sentence and the confiscation of your car. Random drink-driving checks operate and the minimum fine is in the region of Fr2,000 to Fr30,000

7. In some built-up areas, the *priorité à droite* rule applies and will be signposted. In this case you should give way to vehicles joining your road from the right. However, this rule no longer applies at roundabouts and you must give way to vehicles already on the island – ie those approaching from your left. The sign you will see on approaching the island is, *'Vous n'avez pas la priorité'* or *'Cedez la passage'*, which means, 'Give way'.

8. Speed limits (see also below), if broken, can earn an on-the-spot fine. Speeding fines are in the region of Fr300 to Fr5,000. Speed limits in built-up areas begin as soon as the name-plate of the town or village is shown. *'Rappel'* means 'Slow down' and is often prior warning of a lower speed limit, say when approaching a bend or other road hazard.

Speed limits

Autoroutes/(A) roads – 130kph (81mph) in dry weather; 110kph (68mph) in wet weather or when there is poor visibility.

National Routes/(N) roads – 110kph (68mph) in dry weather; 90kph (56mph) in wet weather or when there is poor visibility.

Other roads/(D) roads – outside built-up areas 90kph (56mph) in dry weather; 80kph (50mph) in wet weather or when there is poor visibility.

Towns – 50/60kph (31/37mph). The speed limit in towns varies according to road width and other factors and will be signposted.

Parking

Despite appearances, there are rules governing parking in French towns. By-laws vary from place to place and, in market towns, from day to day. Parking in some streets is permitted on one side on odd dates, and on the other side on even dates. Many places have parking meters (*horodateurs*), but these are usually only for short stay parking; other towns have parking discs which you can obtain at the tourist office. Some car parks have a barrier which opens when a paid-up ticket is fed into a slot.

Preparing the car before driving in France

1. Buy spare bulbs and a spare fan belt, and perhaps a spare accelerator and clutch cables.

2. Make sure the car has been serviced recently.

3. Check the brakes and condition of the tyres – tyre wear rules are similar to those in the UK. Check fluid levels in the brake and clutch reservoirs and make sure the battery acid level covers each cell.

4. Make sure all tyre pressures are correct, including the spare, especially if the car is going to be fully loaded with passengers and luggage.

5. Check the anti-freeze content of the radiator. This is not so strange a tip as it may seem. Anti-freeze raises the boiling point of water and will help to prevent boiling, a common cause of vehicle breakdown in hot weather. Check that any hoses have not become soggy and check whether any clips need replacing.

6. Carry spare fuel in a can (this is legal in France). Have a few useful odds and ends like insulating tape, jump leads, a tow rope and a fire extinguisher. Carry enough tools to make small repairs, such as tightening cables, nuts and screws, and ensure that the jack will lift the car and that the wheel nuts are not too tight.

7. Finally, always carry a first aid kit and learn the basic first aid rules. This could save lives.

To hire a car

Toll-free numbers in France are:
Citer: 05 05 10 11
Avis: 05 05 22 11
Hertz: 05 05 33 11
Euro Rent: 05 33 22 11
Eurocar: 05 10 05 05

Useful telephone numbers

An English language update on French motorway conditions is available from Autoroute Information by dialling: (00 33) 1 47 05 90 01 from outside France, or 1 47 05 90 01 within France. Traffic information is broadcast on the radio on 89.2 or 107.7FM daily.

AA Roadwatch - *UK calls are charged at 39p per minute cheap rate; 49p per minute at other times*: Continental Roadwatch: 0336 401 904. For traffic conditions to and from ferry ports and major European events; other continental information.

Motoring Abroad (country by country) – France: 0336 401 869. For laws, paperwork, driving conditions, etc.

Continental Roadwatch: 0336 401 884. For French motorways toll information
European fuel prices and availability: 0336 401 884
Port information – Hants/Dorset: 0336 401 891
Kent: 0336 401 890
European weather forecasts – France: 0336 401 107

Health for travellers

EC rules allow British travellers to enjoy the same health care as French citizens. Before leaving Britain you should obtain Form E111 from the Post Office (this is available to anyone with an NHS registration number). The Department of Health booklet *Health Advice to Travellers* explains how to get medical assistance under the French system. The booklet covers what you must pay for and how to reclaim refundable charges, and is available from your doctor's surgery. Chemist shops (*pharmacies*) are marked with a green cross and can often deal with minor ailments and injuries, or give advice about where to go for additional help.

What to do in an emergency

For emergency assistance, dial 17 for the police, 18 for the fire brigade, and unless another number is given for ambulances (usually on a notice at head height, above the telephone in public booths), dial 17 and ask for police assistance. Most call boxes have emergency and other information in English as well as other European languages.

In the case of a motoring accident, you should inform your insurer's French agent (the address is usually provided by your insurer together with an International Accident Report Form).

Messages about emergencies at home

Persons touring abroad can be informed of serious illness in their family courtesy of the BBC World Service. In an emergency, RAC Travel Information at Croydon (tel: 01345 333222) will arrange for a message to be transmitted to the relevant country.

BBC Worldwide Service broadcasts

The BBC broadcasts worldwide in English 24 hours a day. World news is broadcast on the hour on the following frequencies (in kHz):
Northern France
05.00-07.30 hrs – 6195, 3955, 648
07.30-16.00 hrs – 12095, 9760, 648
16.00-22.30 hrs – 12095, 9410, 6195

Southern France
05.00-07.30 hrs – 9410, 6195, 3955
07.30-16.00 hrs – 15070, 12095, 9760
16.00-22.30 hrs – 12095, 9410, 6195

Telephoning the UK from France

Delete the first zero of the number you are calling. Begin by dialling 1944, then the rest of the number minus the first zero; ie to dial a UK number, say (01234) 5679890, dial 19 44 1234 567890.

Most call boxes use cards (*télécartes*), which can be bought at post offices or tobacconists' shops. Post offices are usually open 08.00-19.00 Monday-Friday and 08.00-12.00 on Saturday. Away from the larger towns they may close for about 1^{1}/$_{2}$ hours at lunchtime.

CONVERSION CHART

1 kilogramme (1,000 grams) = 2.2 lbs
1 litre = 1^{3}/$_{4}$ pints
4.5 litres = 1 gallon
1.6 kilometres = 1 mile
1.094 metres = 1 yard
1 hectare = 2^{1}/$_{2}$ acres (approx)
20 °C = 68 °F = (°C x 1.8) + 32

WALKING IN THE LOIRE VALLEY

Walking is a popular sport in France and most of the footpath network, especially the well used paths, is kept reasonably clear and is properly waymarked. Waymarking for the *Grande Randonnée* (GR), long distance footpaths is by white/red horizontal stripes, and sometimes the route number in black. Local routes are waymarked with yellow stripes, or other coloured symbols. A waymark turned through a right-angle means turn right (or left) at the next junction. If it has a line or cross drawn through it, the meaning is 'do not go this way'; in this case look for another waymark nearby, showing the correct route. Orange waymarks indicate bridleways or mountain bike (VTT in French) trails.

There are four main GR long distance trails in the Loire area: the GR3 follows the Loire Valley for 275 km (170 miles). The GR41 meanders 51 km (32 miles) along the Cher Valley. The Indre Valley GR46 is 125 km (78 miles) long; and the GR48 explores 203 km (126 miles) of footpaths in the Creuse and Gartempe valleys.

Variants have a letter added after the number – eg GR3(a). Several of the walks described in this guide use sections of the GRs, which are marked on the route maps.

Using this guide

The walks in this guide are relatively short and are suitable for family groups and individuals of all ages. Most start conveniently from car parks or near good roadside parking. Mention is made of nearby restaurants or food shops where you can buy everything for a picnic.

Public toilets are few and far between in rural France, but it is normally acceptable to use bar or café facilities, especially if you make a small purchase.

Almost all the walks in this guide are predominantly on clearly defined paths or quiet by-lanes. If in any doubt when using this guide, always return to the last recognisably described feature and check again.

The grading of the walks is as follows:

Easy – fairly straightforward terrain with only slight inclines.

Moderate – as above, but with one or two steady climbs.

Strenuous – some steep climbs and descents on open hillsides.

Clothing

Boots are not essential for any of these walks, except after prolonged periods of heavy rain, but strong footwear should be worn. Walking boots or similar are safer on stony paths and are more comfortable on longer walks. Wear lightweight clothing, making sure it will protect your neck and limbs from the sun, and wear a sun hat to protect your face. A light waterproof and a sweater carried in a rucksack will guard against an unexpected change in the weather. Also carry a small first aid kit which should contain an insect repellent, and a water-based drink to prevent dehydration.

Simple rules for walking in the Loire Valley

1. Walk on the left-hand side of the road to face oncoming traffic.
2. Take your time. Hopefully the weather will be warmer than you are normally used to, and in any case you could miss some interesting scenery or pretty views by rushing.
3. Before setting out, tell someone about your plans for the day. Some of the walks are in fairly remote areas.

4. Unless they are already open, close all gates after going through them.
5. Take care not to destroy growing crops, including grass for hay, by keeping to the recognised route.
6. Protect wildlife – do not pick wild flowers or disturb nesting birds.
7. If it rains, be careful on muddy paths, especially when going downhill.
8. Do not try to make friends with farm dogs; their one purpose in life is to act as guardians!
9. Rabies is endemic in France and domestic animals are usually vaccinated. While the chances of humans contracting the disease are very slim, avoid contact with wild animals, especially if they are acting strangely.
10. Lock car doors and make sure that all windows are closed. As in Britain, theft from unattended cars is a major problem in France.

HOTELS AND CAMPING

Hotels are classified by the French Government 'star ratings', which range from the top 'four star-L', through three lower grades to the 'one star' category. Stars are awarded on the basis of the number of bedrooms and facilities, but do not necessarily indicate any recommendation of quality. In fact one and two star family-run hotels are frequently better places to stay than impersonal high class establishments.

All hotels are obliged to show their room rates, which are per room and not for each person. Many smaller hotels include breakfast in the room rate. If the hotel has a restaurant, a menu will be on display either beside the entrance or next to the reception desk. Unless you have booked in advance, it is normal practice to examine the room before agreeing to take it.

Hotel bookings can be made through the local tourist office (*Syndicat d'Initiative*), which may make a small charge (see page 10 for addresses).

The *Bienvenue à la Ferme* label, on the silhouette of a butterfly at the entrance to a farm, indicates that it offers rooms and board vetted by the Gîtes de France organisation. Not only will the accommodation and food be of a high standard, but the farm will also have recreational facilities and will be in an attractive setting. Children will be welcome and are often encouraged to help with the animals.

Gîtes d'Hôtes or *Chambres d'Hôtes* (bed and breakfasts) are an inexpensive form of accommodation. Frequently in private houses, they are a pleasant way of getting to know the local people. Many visitors prefer to self-cater and the range of rented accommodation is enormous, ranging from châteaux to simple farmhouses or rural cottages known as *gîtes*.

Camping can be pre-booked through a holiday company, or just turn up at one of the well-equipped touring sites in the Loire. Many of the sites have shops, swimming pools, hot showers and sports facilities.

Publications giving useful information for booking holiday accommodation

Logis de France – lists reasonably priced family-run hotels. Available from bookshops or the French Government Tourist Office (UK address below).

Châteaux Accueil – details of châteaux owners offering accommodation. Available from bookshops or the French Government Tourist Office.

French Country Welcome – 14,000 B&B addresses; available from bookshops or Gîtes de France (UK address below).

Guide Michelin (Red Guide) – comprehensive information about towns and places to visit, as well as hotel and restaurant recommendations. Also lists garage telephone numbers. Available from bookshops.

Gault Millau – restaurant guide; available from bookshops.

LOCAL TOURIST OFFICES

The following are the main tourist offices in or near places mentioned in this guide. Write to the *Office de Tourisme* at one of the following addresses.

Comité Départemental du Tourisme de Cher
10 Rue de la Chappe
18014 BOURGES Cedex. Tel: 48 65 31 01

Comité Départemental du Tourisme de Loiret
2 Rue de la Bretonnerie
45000 ORLEANS. Tel: 38 54 83 83.

Comité Départemental du Tourisme de Loir-et-Cher
11 Place du Château
41000 BLOIS. Tel: 54 78 55 50

Comité Départemental du Tourisme d'Indre-et-Loire
16 Rue de Buffon
37032 TOURS Cedex. Tel: 47 61 61 23

Comité Départemental du Tourisme de Maine-et-Loire
Place Kennedy
BP 214849021 ANGERS Cedex. Tel: 41 88 23 85

Comité Départemental du Tourisme de Loire-Atlantique
Place du Commerce
44000 NANTES. Tel: 4089 50 77

Nearly all towns have a *Syndicat d'Initiative* which will have details of accommodation and events in the area.

FURTHER USEFUL ADDRESSES

French Government Tourist Office
178 Piccadilly
London W1V 0AL. Tel: (0171) 491 7622

Gîtes de France
c/o French Government Tourist Office, address as above.

Chambres d'Hôtes
Maison des Gîtes de France
35 Rue Godot de Mayroy
75009 Paris. Tel: (1) 47 42 25 43

Logis de France
83 Avenue d'Italie
75013 Paris. Tel: (1) 45 84 70 00

Féderation Français de la Randonnée Pédestre
64 Rue de Gergovie
75014 Paris. Tel: (1) 45 45 31 02

France Information Line
Tel: (0891) 244123
Free motorway maps, reference guide, etc. *Calls cost 49p per minute peak pate; 39p per minute off-peak.*

French Railways Ltd (SNCF)
179 Piccadilly
London W1V 0AB. Tel: (0171) 409 3518

Brittany Ferries
The Brittany Centre
Wharf Road
Portsmouth PO2 8RU
Tel: (01705) 827701 – ferry reservations
(01705) 751833 – inclusive holiday reservations

Brittany Ferries are also at:
Millbay
Plymouth PL1 3EW
Tel: (01752) 221321 – ferry reservations
(01752) 263388 – inclusive holiday reservations

Walk 1
LA CELLE-SUR-LOIRE

5 km (3 miles)   Easy

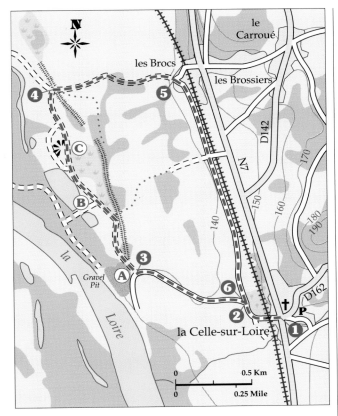

Route description

1 Cross the main road opposite the church with care. Go down the side road, over a level crossing, then bear right on a surfaced lane past a horticultural nursery on the left and orchards to your right.

2 Fork left at the lane junction and walk on beyond the scattered houses, then between meadows where the lane becomes an unsurfaced track.

3 When the track enters a gravel pit, turn right away from the pit, along a fairly wide track through natural woodland. Ignoring side tracks for 1½ km (a little under a mile), follow the main track in and out of scrub woodland.

4 Turn right at the T-junction, past a rather futile flood barrier embankment. Ignore a second path to the right and continue ahead on the wider track, still through woodland.

5 Turn right on reaching the hamlet of les Brocs to follow a surfaced lane parallel to the railway line, on its right-hand side. Walk beside fields and over the next crossroads.

6 Bear left when you reach the outward bound lane, then left again to follow it over the level crossing and back to the main road and the centre of la Celle.

Points of interest

A Sand and gravel borne by the River Loire is quarried for building purposes.

B Side tracks, on either side of attractively naturalised abandoned gravel pits, lead through scrub woodland and down to the river bank. This is an ideal place to look for a picnic spot.

C Viewpoint. The twin cooling towers downstream in the distance are part of the nuclear electric power station at Neuvy-sur-Loire.

This walk can make a pleasant break from driving along the busy N7, the road following the north bank of the Loire. It is especially suited for a walk prior to a picnic lunch, which can be enjoyed in the woods bordering the river.

The route is easy to follow and uses lanes and tracks through meadows and natural woodland where the locals often wander of an evening or at weekends. There is ample opportunity to divert towards the tree-lined river bank. The nearest town with a broad selection of shops is Cosne-sur-Loire, but there are one or two village stores and a bakery in la Celle, as well as roadside cafés and restaurants quite handy to the village.

How to get there: La Celle-sur-Loire is astride the N7, about 7 km (4 1/4 miles) to the north of Cosne-sur-Loire. Park near the church in the centre of the village (on the right of the main road if approaching from the direction of Cosne-sur-Loire).

Walk 2
SANCERRE'S VINEYARDS

6 km (3¾ miles)   Moderate

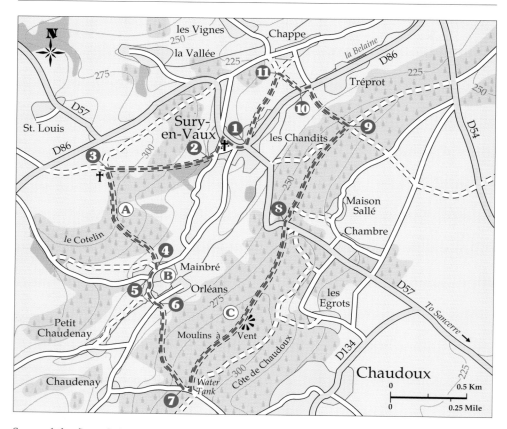

Some of the finest Loire vintages are grown in the small vineyards surrounding Sancerre and its neighbour, Pouilly-sur-Loire. Sancerre is above the west bank of the Loire, whereas Pouilly is a few miles upstream on the opposite bank.

The sleepy hilltop town of Sancerre overlooks clusters of tiny villages, *dômaines* and small farms whose vineyards produce wines bearing the illustrious Sancerre *appellation,* which is internationally renowned. Below the town, the Loire follows its languid course towards the sea. You will need great determination if you intend to ignore the offer of wine tastings (*dégustations*) as you pass the vineyards on the walk.

Sury-en-Vaux is typical of the Sancerre villages, providing a focal point for a number of inter-linked hamlets which depend for their livelihood on the degree of success or failure of each year's grape harvest. The village of Sury-en-Vaux sits in a 'fold' in the chalk downland, about 5 km (3 miles) north-west of Sancerre.

Using tracks that are centuries old, this walk explores a number of vineyards on either side of a deep cut valley that separates the Sury vineyards from those above the village of Chaudoux to the south. The walk involves two climbs; one out of Sury-en-Vaux and the other from Mainbré up to the vine covered ridge of the Côte de Chaudoux. You get a good view from the ridge of the terraces of carefully tended vines.

There is a small bar/restaurant in Sury-en-Vaux offering good plain food, but for anything more elaborate, Sancerre has a wide range of high class restaurants as well as a number of small cafés and shops.

How to get there: Take the D54 from Sancerre, across the D955 Bourges road, to Fontenay. From here continue along the D54 until it forks, then follow the D57 via Chambre into Sury-en-Vaux. Park in the village centre.

Take care at the sharp right-hand hairpin bend going downhill, about 500 metres (a third of a mile) beyond Chambre.

Route description

❶ From the central square in Sury-en-Vaux, walk towards the church and turn left along a narrow side road called the Avenue des Vines.

❷ Where the surfaced road bears left, turn right and go steeply uphill along a cart track to the right of a small wood. Climb towards the upper limits of the vine covered slopes beyond the wood.

❸ Turn left at a four-way track junction marked by a wayside cross and begin to go downhill, first across the slope of the hill, then more steeply downhill through a series of vineyards. Go through a couple of lower meadows and into the tiny hamlet of Mainbré.

❹ Turn right and follow the road along the valley bottom for about 100 metres through Mainbré, until it forks.

❺ Take the left fork and follow the narrow road past scattered cottages and tiny fields, then over a small stream.

❻ Ignore the lane to your left beyond the bridge, and where the road swings sharply right, continue ahead on a cart track which climbs steeply uphill through meadowland, then between north-west facing vine-yards. Ignore side tracks until you reach a wide pass between two broad chalk ridges.

❼ Walk forwards along the surfaced road for two or three metres then turn left in front of a covered hilltop water storage tank. Follow the crest of the vine covered ridge, gently uphill at first, then steadily downhill. Take the left fork above the surfaced road.

❽ Cross the D57 above the sharp hairpin bend. Continue ahead along the rough track opposite, going gently downhill between a series of small vine-yards. Walk on where another track joins from the left.

❾ Turn left at the crosstracks to go steeply downhill. Turn left on reaching the valley bottom road and proceed for about 80 metres, past a group of buildings.

❿ Turn right and follow a side track dog-legging slightly uphill next to a series of small fields.

⓫ Turn sharp left at a four-way track junction to follow a tree-lined rural lane back to the centre of Sury-en-Vaux.

Points of interest

Ⓐ Take a little time to study the way the vines have been carefully pruned each autumn and how the new growth is trained along taut wires stretched between angled poles. Strange looking, specially adapted tractors might be within sight, keeping the vines free of weeds.

Ⓑ A number of wine growers in Mainbré offer tastings (*dégustations*) in hope that you will buy some of their bottles.

Ⓒ Viewpoint. Below you are the wine-growing villages of Verdigny, Chaudoux, les Egrots and Chambre. Further in the distance, Sancerre is visible on the top of the hill, a position that was once important for defence. Ridge-top windmills used to harness the winds passing over the Côte de Chaudoux, but modern methods of milling corn have led to the abandonment of this industry. Only a few stones mark the site of these erstwhile important features in the land-scape.

Walk 3
LE VAL DE BEAULIEU
6 km (3¾ miles)   Easy

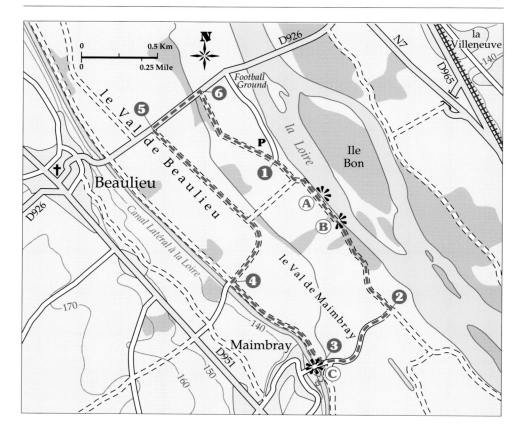

This is a gentle stroll along river and canal-side tracks on what is effectively a man-made island created by the Canal Latéral à la Loire. Roughly paralleling the Loire, the canal was dug in the 19th century to enable water-borne traffic to move up and down the valley throughout the year. Prior to its contruction, low water levels of the Loire in the summer prevented the movement of heavy goods. The canal superseded an inefficient road system, but as with most other canals, competition from the railways caused its commercial death. Today mostly pleasure craft may be seen cruising the water lily padded waters of the Canal Latéral à la Loire.

The walk is within easy distance of the small rural town of Beaulieu. Its medieval town centre is traffic free – a delightful place to wander and explore hidden by-ways. Beaulieu has a solidly built ancient church, notable for the barge-like pews that fill its nave.

Fortunately, Bonny-sur-Loire, on the opposite side of the river, may be by-passed by a loop of the N7, for the town is quieter as a result. Although a pleasant town, it is more industrialised than Beaulieu, and is therefore less of a backwater.

There is a good selection of shops, cafés and restaurants in both Beaulieu and Bonny-sur-Loire, which should cater for all tastes and pockets.

How to get there: Access to the start of the walk is off the D926 which links the N7 at Bonny-sur-Loire with Beaulieu. If approaching from Bonny, turn sharp left about 120 metres after crossing the river bridge. Coming from Beaulieu, follow the N926 below the town for 1 km (a little over half of a mile) beyond the canal. Take the second turning on the right after passing through a wooded belt, where the road starts to climb up to the bridge over the Loire. Drive down the unsurfaced side lane past a football ground and park near a small factory making cement-based building materials. There is plenty of space for parked cars, but make sure you do not get in the way of lorries entering or leaving the factory.

Route description

❶ Follow the level unsurfaced riverside track through meadows and beside rough woodland. Ignore a side track to the right about 250 metres after leaving the factory site and continue along the main track which twists left, closer to the river.

❷ Turn sharp right at the track junction, away from the river. Follow what soon becomes a narrow surfaced lane winding its way through fields towards higher ground.

❸ On reaching a bridge over the canal, do not cross over but turn right. Go down to the towpath and follow it past a little used grain silo on the opposite bank. Continue as far as the next bridge.

❹ Climb up to the bridge and turn right, away from the canal, then go slightly downhill along a woodland track. Follow the track out into open fields and around a sweeping left-hand bend. Ignore the side track on the right about 200 metres beyond the bend, and walk on until you reach the road between Bonny-sur-Loire and Beaulieu.

❺ Turn right to follow the road for 350 metres between fields then through a narrow belt of trees on either side of a small stream.

❻ Turn right onto the track marking the far boundary of the woodland. Follow it towards, then around the building materials factory, back to where you parked the car.

Points of interest

Ⓐ Viewpoint. Fishermen's paths to the left of the track meander through the dense trees lining the Loire to the river bank, where there are attractive views up and downstream. Directly opposite, the low-lying Ile Bon is often partly submerged in early spring. This occurs when snow on the Auvergne mountains melts and floods down the valley.

Ⓑ Viewpoint, looking towards the distant cooling towers of the nuclear electric power station at Neuvy-sur-Loire. It may be possible to visit the plant, but check first for opening details at a local tourist office.

Ⓒ Viewpoint. The canal bridge overlooks one of the locks on the Canal Latéral à la Loire, where the accordian playing lock keeper often serenades waiting pleasure cruisers. The canal is part of the extensive inland water network criss-crossing France, and follows the Loire upstream towards the Massif Central. Downstream at Briare, where the Latéral begins, it is possible to follow its sister canal, the Canal de Briare, as far as the River Seine at Moret-sur-Loing, and from there to continue on the river into Paris.

Walk 4
PIERREFITTE-ES-BOIS

8.5 km (5¼ miles)   Easy

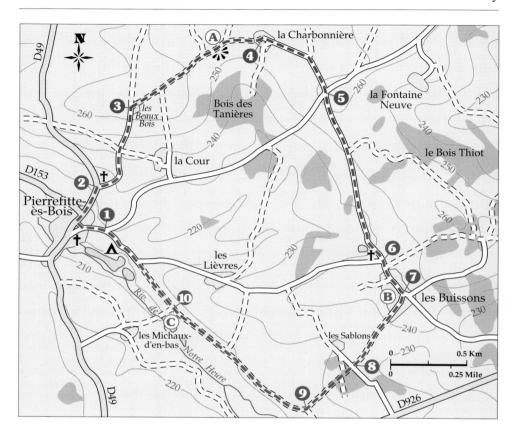

Pierrefitte-ès-Bois is one of those tiny out-of-the-way places where time is measured in decades and the cares of the rest of the world seem quite meaningless. The village stands a little to the north-west of the Sancerre vineyards, and concentrates more on dairy farming than vine growing.

The focal point of this walk is a secluded pond-side campsite on the outskirts of the village. The route follows quiet back lanes and field tracks around lush farmland and through shaded oak woods and other broad-leaved woodland. There is a small château a little to one side of the lanes leading out of the village, and in its centre is a venerable old church.

The only source of refreshment is in the tiny *bar-tabacs* where the locals congregate. Otherwise, you can make up a picnic from purchases at the bakery and general store.

How to get there: Pierrefitte-ès-Bois is at the junction of the D49 and D153, about 15 km (9 miles) south of Briare by way of Châtillon-sur-Loire. Unless you are staying at the campsite, park in the lay-by on the opposite side of the road from the entrance to the site.

Route description

1 From the campsite, walk along the road into the village, aiming for the slender spire of Pierrefitte-ès-Bois' church. Walk through the centre of the village and turn right along the Châtillon-sur-Loire/Briare road, the D49. Bear right with the D49 where the D153 Cernoy-en-Berry road forks left.

2 Leave the main road by turning right onto a quiet shaded side lane marked by a wayside cross and signposted to les Beaux Bois. Follow the lane steadily uphill and over a minor crossroads.

3 Turn right at the farmhouse, but keep the buildings on your right to follow a grassy cart track over a slight rise. Ignore a side track to the right at the top of the rise and begin to go gently downhill along the tree-lined track, between meadowland and cultivated fields. Bear right at the next two track junctions and continue until you reach the farming hamlet of la Charbonnière.

4 Follow the surfaced lane to the right and away from la Charbonnière, then walk between hedges bordering rolling open fields.

5 Walk ahead over the crossroads and follow the quiet tree and hedge-lined country road gently downhill between meadows and small clumps of woodland.

6 Continue ahead at the road junction marked by a wayside shrine and into the tiny village of les Buissons.

7 Just before a side road on the left leaves the main road, turn right and walk past scattered groups of houses and then into a farmyard. Leave the farmyard by following a rough cart track past occasional clumps of trees and through open meadows and cultivated fields.

8 Cross a side lane giving access to the little farming community of les Sablons and enter a small wood. Follow the track through the wood, ignoring other tracks on either side. Continue along a tree-lined track on the far side of the wood.

9 Turn right at a T-junction to follow a narrow track through fields a little way above a meandering tree-shaded stream, the Heure. Continue forwards along a level field path where another track climbs uphill to the right. Part of this section of the path is in a shallow cutting and may be muddy after prolonged wet weather.

10 Walk on along the gradually improving track which has joined your path from the left, and still keeping well to the right and above the stream, follow it back to the road. Turn left along the road to return to Pierrefitte-ès-Bois and the campsite.

Points of interest

A Viewpoint looking south across rolling green countryside towards the vineyards of Sancerre. In the far distance, more vineyards of the Pouilly vintages can be faintly glimpsed above the opposite bank of the Loire. Closer to hand, below and to the right of the large wood in the foreground, the pretty farm/château of la Cour completes an idyllic scene.

B Les Buissons is an unspoilt farming community, which is typical of the rural hinterland bordering the Loire valley.

C Ponds in the valley bottom once provided the motive power to drive local flour mills. They also acted as fishponds to augment the sparse diet of past times. Today locals and visitors alike can enjoy a pleasant shaded hour or so angling for the wily carp that live in these muddy waters.

Walk 5
AUTRY-LE-CHATEL

6 km (3¾ miles)   Easy

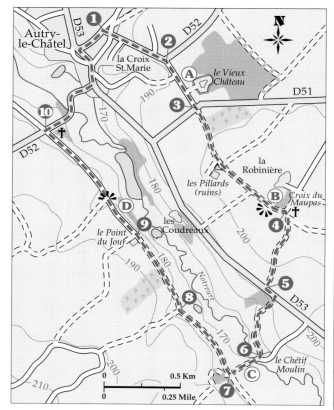

This sleepy village sits astride the D53 to the south-west of forests bordering the distant Loire. Autry-le-Châtel has survived long after its château was abandoned.

Small bars near the central square offer food and you will be rewarded by the friendly chatter of local characters. There are, however, the usual village shops and the almost 'English' atmosphere of the village green at the start of the walk makes it an ideal picnic spot.

How to get there: The D53 leaves the D940 Gien to Argent-sur-Sauldre road at a busy crossroads about 6 km (3³/4 miles) south-west of Gien. Autry is a further 6 km south along the D53. Park beside the village green, beyond the cemetery and opposite the fire station (*Caserne de Pompiers*).

Route description

1 From the green, turn right and follow the D52 away from the fire station, where it is signposted to Châtillon-sur-Loire, St. Brisson and the *Vieux Château*.

2 Bear right at the junction, along an unclassified side road past the old château.

3 Cross the D51 and continue ahead on a white hard-surfaced cart track, going gently uphill. Go past a small pond and a group of ruined farm buildings. Ignore side turnings into nearby fields.

4 Continue ahead across the top of a T-junction marked by a wayside cross. After about 50 metres, bear right with another track junction and proceed to the main road.

5 Turn left and walk along the road beside a wood and to its far side. Turn right and follow the edge of the wood downhill along a tree-shaded track between meadows. Join the end of a minor side road and turn right to cross a bridge.

6 Walk uphill on the tree-shaded track at the far side of the stream.

7 Turn right at the crosstracks and follow a terraced grassy track below the level of the upper fields. Follow the river downstream.

8 Bear right at the track junction to climb a little and then go under electicity power lines.

9 Continue ahead on the steadily improving side lane above small woodlands and a large pond.

10 On reaching the road, turn right at a wayside cross. Follow the road across the valley and turn left into the centre of Autry.

Points of interest

A Visitors are not welcome at the old château, but you can see most of the building from the roadside. Beyond an algae-filled moat, the drive leads through an arched gateway.

B Viewpoint looking across the Notreure valley to a pastoral scene of farmlands and woods.

C The tiny bridge serves as an attractive resting place.

D Viewpoint looking across the millpond towards Autry.

18

Walk 6
BRIARE AND ITS CANALS

5 km (3 miles)   Easy

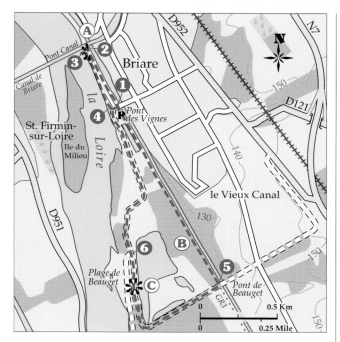

Briare grew as a commercial town around the inland port which stands at the junction of two major canal routes. Before the railway and road networks were developed, rivers such as the Loire were the commercial arteries of France. However, shallows on either side of Briare made it difficult to manoeuvre craft along this part of the Loire, so to avoid the bottleneck, a short length of canal was dug. Subsequently the canal system was expanded, effectively linking the four corners of France, and the rivers Loire and Seine were linked by the Canal de Briare. Meanwhile, the Canal Latéral à la Loire carried goods between the Massif Central and the more populated centres of the north. The two canals still carry a small amount of commercial traffic, but pleasure craft now prevail.

The walk visits both the old and 'new' canals, using part of the GR3 long distance footpath, and it uses a riverside path much favoured by local strollers.

There are no refreshment facilities en route, but nearby Briare has a good selection of shops, bars and restaurants of all kinds.

How to get there: From the town centre in Briare, follow the main road, the D952, in the direction of Bonny-sur-Loire. Cross the Briare canal and drive on for a little over half a kilometre (a third of a mile). Turn right along the side street, Rue Georges Charpenet, which is signposted to the Bordes de Loire. Go past the houses and

park beside the play park at the Pont des Vignes.

Route description

❶ Follow the canal towpath back in the direction of Briare.

❷ Climb to the right up to the road bridge over the Briare Canal. Do not cross it but turn left along its towpath as far as the start of the aqueduct.

❸ Turn left and go down a flight of iron steps from the aqueduct in order to reach the river embankment. Turn left again and walk upstream.

❹ Turn left and walk up to the canal bridge, the Pont des Vignes, then turn right and follow the towpath.

❺ Turn right at the bridge and leave the canal. Walk down the access track to an old gravel pit. Follow the track around flooded abandoned pits now naturalised by maturing willows. Bear right at their limit and walk downstream through scrub woodland above the banks of the Loire.

❻ Bear right at a track junction and follow the steadily improving track back to the car park.

Points of interest

Ⓐ Viewpoint. The magnificent aqueduct of Pont Canal was built by Alexander Gustave Eiffel (who is, of course, better known for his design of the Eiffel Tower) between 1890 and 1894.

Ⓑ The towpath is part of the GR3, a long distance footpath that follows a 275 km (170 mile) route along the Loire valley.

Ⓒ Viewpoint. The nearby woodlands, river bank and gravel pits attract a wide variety of bird life. To your left through the trees, the sandy beach is a popular picnic place.

19

Walk 7
SENTIER DES SOURCES

Up to 7 km (4¼ miles) Easy/Moderate

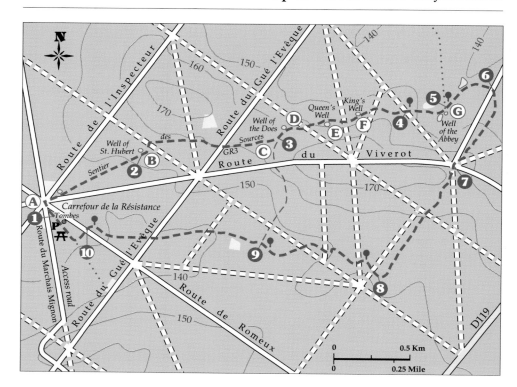

Near the centre of the dense woodland of the *Forêt Domaniale d'Orléans* to the north-west of Gien, two roofless houses stand next to a war memorial, shaded by groups of massive sequoia trees. It is hard to believe that this tranquil spot was once the scene of an horrific skirmish when a group of French Resistance fighters *(maquisards)* were ambushed by German troops.

On 14th August 1944, the Frenchmen were trapped in one of the few clearings in the forest. Unable to return accurate firepower or effect an escape, most of the *maquisards* were slaughtered; those who were captured were executed on the spot, and others were hunted down in the surrounding undergrowth.

Leading those who fell on that fateful day, and one of the few to escape, was the part Irish adventurer, Lt. Col. Marc O'Neill. He was awarded the *Legion de l'Honneur* and the O.B.E. for his work in organising French resistance in the Loire region, and went on to serve France in North Africa, where he was killed during the Algerian crisis in 1956. His body was brought back to France to be buried alongside his resistance comrades at the forest memorial. The names of those who lie there, and those of individuals buried where they fell, are carved on the simple plinth.

The forest is a carefully managed area of natural woodland where magnificent specimen trees have grown to a great height. Forest rides and fire breaks, cut at regular angles, have divided the forest into numerous irregular blocks. Wildlife abounds, from deer, badgers and wild boar, to tiny woodland birds. The forestry service has ensured that no part of the woodland has been allowed to become so dense as to prevent ground cover. As a result, shade-loving flowers and creepers flourish in the undergrowth.

A waymarked path, the *Sentier des Sources*, leaves the Resistance Memorial, and guided by yellow waymarks, winds its way around various sections of nearby forest. Several specimen trees are passed along the way, plus the six wells or *'sources'*, which give this walk its title.

As there is nowhere to buy refreshments during the walk, a picnic should be carried. The nearest shops are at Ouzouer-sur-Loire and there are picnic tables near the car park where the walk starts.

The château of Sully-sur-Loire is nearby on the opposite side of the Loire and it can easily be visited either before or after the walk. The town of Sully and its château were badly damaged during World War II, but have been carefully restored. The fortress-like château sits above the Loire, to one side of the town, and is surrounded by a large moat. Dating from the 14th century and with one of the finest timber roofs in Europe, it once held the captive Joan of Arc. The old part of Sully is also worth exploring. Its collegiate Church of St. Ythier contains some fine 16th-century stained glass.

Dampierre Nuclear Power Station is occasionally open to visitors should you wish to contrast the ancient château with 20th-century industry. It is advisable to check opening details with a local tourist office.

How to get there: To reach the start of the walk, follow the D119 Montereau road north-east from Ouzouer-sur-Loire (where it links with the D952 Loire Valley road) for a little over 2 km (1¼ miles). Turn left at the signpost to the *Monument de la Résistance* and drive for just over 4 km (2½ miles) along an unsurfaced forest road as far as a traffic island marked by a group of huge sequoia trees. Leave the car in the signposted car park on the right.

Route description

❶ From the car park, walk towards the war memorial and turn right, away from the forest road. Go past the ruined forestry house and the first well, following a path marked by yellow waymarks.

❷ Go past the second well head, over a forest ride, then bear right, climbing slightly at first. Cross a wide fire break. Go forwards across an unsurfaced forest road and on to a path juntion.

It is possible to shorten the walk by turning right at this point and following the white/red waymarks to ❾, where another right turn will take you back onto the described route

❸ Bear left at the path junction and follow yellow and white/red waymarks until you reach the next well. Go over three more fire breaks, passing two further wells along the way.

❹ Go over another fire break, marked by a large oak tree, then gently downhill past a small pond beside the sixth well.

❺ Take the right fork beside another large oak and follow the forest path now indicated only by yellow waymarks.

❻ Cross over the unsurfaced forest road to climb the winding path, fairly steeply uphill.

❼ On reaching a road junction, go forwards, and still following the yellow waymarks, start to go downhill.

❽ Bear right and follow the path over the next four fire breaks, passing two specimen oaks.

❾ Go forwards at the path junction, again with white/red as well as yellow waymarks, steadily downhill across two fire breaks.

❿ Pass another oak and cross the forest road. Turn right on joining another path and walk back to the car park.

Points of interest

Ⓐ The names of the fallen resistance fighters and their leader Lt. Col. Marc O'Neill, *Legion de l'Honneur*, O.B.E., are recorded on the simple memorial. The two ruined forestry houses have been left as they were after the battle.

Ⓑ Well of St. Hubert.

Ⓒ White/red waymarks on the path joining from the right indicate that it is a long distance path. This one is the GR3, the 275 km (170 mile) Loire Valley *Grande Randonée*.

Ⓓ Well of the Does.

Ⓔ Queen's Well.

Ⓕ King's Well.

Ⓖ Well of the Abbey.

Walk 8
ST. BENOIT-SUR-LOIRE

6 km (3¾ miles)   Easy

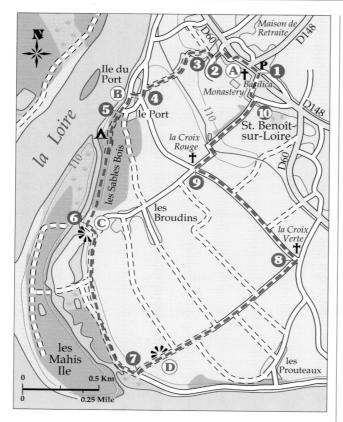

the arts. The surrounding countryside was drained, land was improved and roads and bridges were built, and as a result, the abbey became extremely wealthy. It was so wealthy that, in order to transfer money from place to place, it used Letters of Credit, thereby inventing the banking system. In 1147 Louis VII borrowed money from the Benedictines to finance his Second Crusade, a crusade which ended in disaster for the king.

The abbey's fortunes took a dip during the Wars of Religion between Catholics and Protestants in the 16th century, when it was ransacked and its treasures stolen. Despite a revival in the next century, the Revolution led to the closure of the abbey. However, since the mid-19th century when the abbey of St. Benoît became a national monument, it has been steadily restored. Its architecture is simple Romanesque, and the vaulting and delicate sculpture is quite beautiful. The chancel has a Roman mosaic, and the crypt contains St. Benedict's shrine. Benedictine monks returned after 1945, and since then the abbey has become famous for the tone of its Gregorian chant sung during services.

The village of St. Benoît surrounds the monastery on three sides, well above the flood plain of the Loire. At the ends of the side streets winding haphazardly away from the through roads and the village square, numerous monastic

For centuries pilgrims have come to pray at the abbey of St. Benoît, otherwise known as St. Benedict, the patron saint of Europe and founder of the Benedictine Order. The objects of their devotions are the tombs of St. Benedict and his sister St. Scolastica, whose bodies were brought here from the monastery of Monte Cassino in Italy in the 7th century. A 'strip-cartoon' mural, carved in stone on the lintel above the north door of the basilica church, tells their story.

St. Benoît was a religious site long before the first missionaries converted the locals to Christianity. The early Gauls regarded the area as the spiritual as well as physical centre of their sphere of influence. Thus the 'new' religion, Christianity, took over a ceremonial site used for centuries by the Druids.

Aided by donations from pilgrims, in the Middle Ages St. Benoît became an important centre of learning in both the sciences and buildings, such as the *Maison de Retraite*, can be found, which are linked to the abbey.

St. Benoît has a long history of welcoming visitors, and so has a good range of restaurants and shops.

The nearest châteaux open to the public are at Lorris, Orléans and la Ferté St. Aubin.

How to get there: St. Benoît is to the west of the D952, on the D60 side road linking Châteauneuf-sur-Loire and St. Père-sur-Loire. Park in the central square in St. Benoît, near the *Hôtel de Ville* (town hall).

Route description

❶ Follow signposts away from the town square, to the Basilica Church.

❷ Go past the church and to the right beside the *Hôtel du Labrador*, through the car park then following a narrow surfaced path out towards open fields.

❸ Cross a tiny bridge, walk on for about 80 metres and turn left at the track junction. Follow the track, keeping to the left of a farmhouse.

❹ Climb the embankment and turn left to walk along the lane for 100 metres. Just before the lane forks, turn right along a narrow track down to houses lining the lower road. Turn left and walk through the hamlet of le Port.

❺ When the lane turns sharp left, walk forwards along a track leading to the campsite. Keep left on the main track, then walk on through woodland bordering the Loire. The track gradually narrows to become a footpath.

❻ Turn left onto the river access track, then right where it joins a track on top of an embankment. Follow this past a gravel pit, then with scrub woodland on your right and fields to the left.

❼ Turn left and drop down from the embankment, then walk on along a lane giving access to fields on either side. Ignore side turnings to the right and left.

❽ Turn sharp left at a three-way junction marked by a tiny wayside cross, and follow the lane between fields and meadows.

❾ Go to the right at a crossroads marked by another wayside cross and follow the narrow road, past a small pond and a wood then into the outskirts of St. Benoît.

❿ Bear left then right along side streets to return to the town centre.

Points of interest

Ⓐ The cool interior of the Basilica Church is one of many reasons for entering its hushed precincts. Founded in the Middle Ages, its Benedictine library is one of the finest in France.

Ⓑ The name of this hamlet, Le Port, tells us that in the abbey's heyday, long before the advent of roads and railways, barges laden with goods or pilgrims would tie up beside the embankment here.

Ⓒ Viewpoint looking across a shallow oxbow lake lined with gravel shoals, and the crescent shaped island of les Mahis, towards a broad sweep of the Loire.

Ⓓ Viewpoint. The rich fields and lush pastures are built on land created by draining the ancient flood plain of the River Loire.

Walk 9
CHATEAU DE LA FERTE ST. AUBIN

7 km (4¼ miles)   Easy

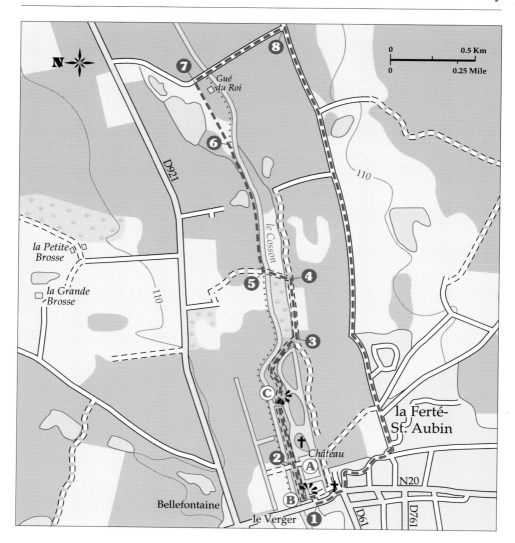

The château is on the northern outskirts of this attractive town. After visiting it, the walk continues alongside the tree-lined stream feeding its moat. A quiet road, tree-shaded for much of the way, leads back through modern housing developments on the outskirts of la Ferté St. Aubin, into the town centre.

There are a number of small restaurants and café/bars in Ferté St. Aubin, as well as shops where food for a picnic can be bought.

In the Domaine Solognot du Ciran, 6 km (3³/4 miles) along the D108 to the east of la Ferté St. Aubin, there is a wildlife park concentrating on regional fauna of the Loire. It is open every day of the year and it takes about 1¹/2 hours walking to traverse the open parkland.

How to get there: Follow the N20 Lamotte-Beuvron road south from Orléans. The Château of la Ferté St. Aubin is on the left immediately after crossing the narrow River Cosson. Park either beside the château entrance or closer to the town centre.

Route description

1 The walk begins at the roadside entrance to the château. Facing the building, take the track ahead and turn left immediately to follow the path around the moat.

2 Keep ahead over a track leading to the château and walk on, still beside the moat, past a chapel on a little island to your right. Continue upstream along the tree-shaded riverside track. Go over a footbridge and bear right away from the main river and towards a feeder stream flowing into the moat.

3 Go over the feeder stream and turn left at a track junction.

4 Turn left at the next track junction, cross the stream and walk forwards towards the main river. Cross the bridge.

5 Turn right and follow a woodland path upstream along the river bank.

6 Fork left beside a small weir and move away from the river, across water meadows and through scrub woodland.

7 Go through a kissing gate and turn right to walk along the woodland road. Climb steadily uphill after crossing the river.

8 Turn right at the crossroads and follow the road, through woodland then beside fields, into the modern outskirts of la Ferté St. Aubin. The town centre and château are to the right on reaching the main road.

Points of interest

A The Château of la Ferté St. Aubin is run by a semi-voluntary society. Its interior has recently been opened to the public and such is their hand-to-mouth existence that it is said that each entry fee pays for four new roof slates!

Founded in the 11th century to guard a crossing of the River Cosson, the château passed through the hands of several noble families before it was inherited in the 16th century by the St. Nectaires. Under their stewardship, the château became known as *la Ferté Senectère* and was modernised to take on its present form. In 1746, in the reign of Louis XV, it was sold to Woldemar of Lowendal, Maréchal of France and great-grandson of Frederick II, King of Denmark. Thereafter the château was owned by various Maréchals and it became known as the Maréchals' château. From 1911 to 1987, it was owned by an Irish family, the O'Gormans. Then it was taken over by Jaques Guyot, who began the mammoth task of restoration. As with most châteaux open to the public, la Ferté contained few of its original furnishings when it was bought by Jaques Guyot. However, careful acquisitions have enabled the furnishing of rooms on three floors in 17th-century style. Children will be particularly interested in the Toy Room and in Pauline's Room, furnished as it would have been for a maid servant. The kitchens, containing massive cooking implements, are also not to be missed.

Whilst there are guided tours, most visitors prefer to wander unaccompanied, following the arrows inside the château.

Outside, the coach house, saddle room and stables are set out as in their heyday, including stabling for two massive Franche-Comté horses. Over the little bridge behind the castle, the château chapel sits on a tiny man-made island.

Flower festivals and other events are held either in the château or in its gardens throughout the summer. Look out for advertised details.

B Viewpoint looking across the water-lily filled moat to the romantic vision of the ancient château.

C Viewpoint looking across the island with its fairy-tale chapel and towards the turreted rear view of the château.

Walk 10
BEAUGENCY

7 km (4¼ miles)   Easy

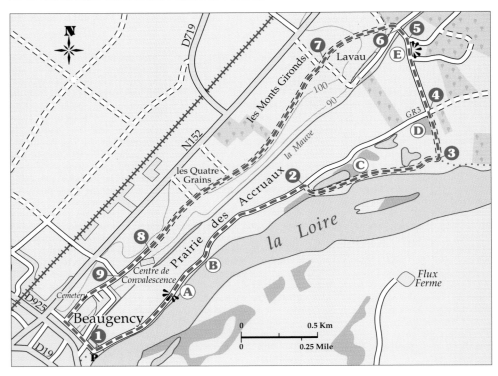

Until modern times, the bridge over the Loire from Beaugency was the only crossing point between Orléans and Blois. Being such an important river crossing and the focal point of major routes between northern and southern France, it commanded a strategically important site. It was fought over during the Hundred Years War, and was captured four times by the English. Only after Joan of Arc relieved Beaugency in 1429 did it come firmly under French control.

Joan of Arc is widely associated with this part of France. In May 1429 she led her army to free Orléans, which was beseiged by the English, but due to an error she arrived on the wrong side of the Loire and had to march downstream to Beaugency before she could cross safely. After a series of sharp battles lasting four days between 4th and 8th May 1429, the English were driven from Orléans, marking a major turning point in the Hundred Years War. Every year on the 7th and 8th May, Orléans celebrates this important victory with a firework festival. Joan of Arc's equestrian statue is in the Place du Martroi in the city centre.

The only other reminder of those turbulent times in Orléans is the ruined castle keep (*donjon*). The adjacent Château Dunois, in the centre of the old town, houses the Musée Régional des Arts et Traditions de l'Orléans, a collection of local costumes covering a span of several centuries.

Exploring the pretty old town of Beaugency is an ideal preliminary to this riverside walk. Narrow streets and overhanging medieval buildings create a pleasantly shaded area. There are organised tours of the old town and Beaugency's château hosts a drama festival every June.

The walk is a popular evening stroll with the locals. It starts by the bridge over the Loire and follows the north bank of the river upstream, before returning by way of orchards, lush fields and meadows. There is a wide variety of restaurants, *crêperies* and small cafés to choose from in the town centre, and a number of excellent *boulangeries, épiceries* and *charcuteries*.

How to get there: Beaugency is on the north side of the Loire on the N152, south-west of Orléans. If you are not staying in the town, the best place to park is in the car park by the riverside, upstream of the bridge, which is convenient to the start of the walk.

Route description

1 Follow the surfaced riverside lane, upstream and away from the bridge for 1½ km (1 mile).

2 Approaching scrub woodland lining the river bank, bear right away from the surfaced lane, onto a rough track through the trees and close to the river. Skirt a series of flooded and abandoned old gravel pits.

3 Turn left at a track junction, away from the river and along a steadily improving track.

4 Go over the crosstracks, forwards along the surfaced lane between orchards and cultivated fields. Continue ahead at the next track junction joining from your right.

5 Bear half left at the following junction and head towards rising ground. Go over a small stream at the foot of the rise.

6 At the T-junction, cross the road then bear half left to follow a narrow grassy field track, uphill to the left of an orchard. Climb into open fields.

7 Ignore the side tracks on the left and right and continue forwards through a series of fields above the ancient flood plain. Go past further orchards, ignoring side tracks on the right and field entrances.

8 Keep walking forwards when the track joins a surfaced lane, and go past a convalescence home.

9 Continue ahead past the road joining from the right. Walk on beyond the cemetery as far as the T-junction at the end of the road. Turn left at the T-junction, and walk downhill, past the football ground on your left, then over the next road junction to reach the riverside car park.

Points of interest

A Viewpoint looking back towards the bridge and Beaugency, dominated by its ancient *donjon* keep.

B The powerboat and sailing club is open to visitors. Kayaking and cycling holidays are also organised locally. Enquire for details from: Loisirs-Accueil-Loiret, 3 Rue da la Bretonnerie, 45000 Orléans. Tel: 38 62 04 88.

C The abandoned flooded gravel pits attract large numbers of rare birds and are also good for coarse fishing. The section of the nearby Loire on the right is slow running and so is also mainly used for coarse fishing. Permits are issued on a *département* basis, usually from local tourist offices, although some fishing tackle shops sell them. Open season is from mid-June to mid-April.

D The track to the right and left is part of the GR3, the long distance footpath route along the Loire Valley.

E Viewpoint overlooking apple orchards. The farms usually sell surplus stock at the roadside.

Walk 11
VALLEE DE LA GRANDE PIERRE   9 km (5½ miles)   Easy/Moderate

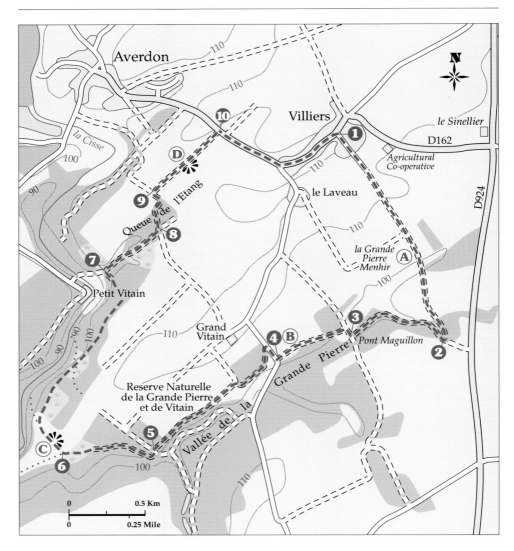

At first glance, the flat countryside on either side of the Loire, especially to the north, can seem lacking in attraction, as there are vast expanses of monotonous farmland. However, it is possible to move away from areas of intensive farming into unspoilt natural woodlands and tiny rural hamlets that will reward the time spent seeking them out.

This walk is an example of what can be found by simply turning off the main road and exploring ancient byways and woodland tracks, in this case not all that far from a large town.

The fertile lands around Blois have been farmed for many centuries, a fact that is highlighted by the enigmatic and lonely standing stone at the head of the valley, the *menhir*, which gives this walk its title. Erected by the prehistoric ancestors of the modern farmers living nearby, its purpose is not known. As with other standing stones scattered around western Europe, the need to transport and erect such a huge stone far from its original site, is open to conjecture. One school of thought suggests that such stones acted as boundary markers or waymarks on ancient cross-country tracks. If this is correct, then the path used on this walk has been followed for several thousand years.

The valley below the *menhir* is a designated nature reserve; its wildlife, both flora and fauna, should therefore be respected. Red squirrels, roe deer and woodland birds are common in the woods and may be seen if you walk quietly and try not to disturb them.

Villiers, the tiny farming community where the walk begins, is an architectural gem, as only a handful of its houses were built in recent years. Cottage gardens and interesting domestic building styles make it a village to savour, and time spent admiring them will be appreciated by the locals provided you are not over-inquisitive.

Unfortunately, there is nowhere offering refreshments en route, but Blois is only 11 km (7 miles) to the south. If you carry a picnic, there will be ample opportunity to enjoy it in one of the shady woodland clearings about half-way along the walk.

How to get there: Drive north along the D924 from Blois and turn left at the Villejambon/Villiers crossroads. Drive on for 1 km (just over half a mile) down the side lane, past the agricultural co-operative, then bear left at a road junction, into Villiers. There is no public car park, so take care not to block anyone's access when parking at the roadside in the centre of the village.

Route description

❶ With your back to the minor junction on the eastern outskirts of Villiers, turn left off the main road (D924), down the side lane called the Chemin de la Grande Pierre. Follow it past farm cottages and when the lane becomes a track, continue between open fields, then gently downhill towards, then across a narrow wooded valley. Climb the short hillside opposite, and then walk on through scrubby woodland, still following the wide track.

❷ On the far side of the wood, turn sharp right at a track junction and begin to go downhill, back into woodland. Bear left with the track on approaching the normally dry valley bottom.

❸ Go to the right on a cart track and cross a small bridge, then turn left onto another track. Walk on through scrubby undergrowth bordering fields.

❹ Turn right on reaching a minor road. Walk slightly uphill for about 80 metres, then turn left to follow a field track along the edge of a wood. Turn left where the track swings right at a junction at the far side of the wood. Continue to walk down the valley, into dense woodland.

❺ Go left, then almost immediately right at a complex track junction. Bear right with the track, and climb gently uphill on the narrowing woodland track. Continue on the path through an area of rough scrub.

❻ Fork right at the path junction. Go downhill and turn right at the next junction. Follow the winding path through woodland, along the east side of the valley of the River Cisse. On entering a clearing, go to the right and steeply downhill where another path bears left. Follow the right-hand path gently uphill and ahead at the next path junction. Walk on through the wood, then swing sharply to the left and steeply downhill on an improving track.

❼ Turn right to follow a woodland track uphill. Ignore any minor side turnings.

❽ Turn left at the crosstracks and walk to the far side of the wood, then follow its boundary.

❾ Turn right at the track junction and walk between fields and meadowland.

❿ Turn right on joining the road, and follow it back into Villiers.

Points of interest

Ⓐ The lonely *menhir* has a decidedly friendly aura in spite of its antiquity.

Ⓑ The valley and surrounding natural woodland have been designated a nature reserve, the *Reserve Naturelle de la Grande Pierre*.

Ⓒ Viewpoint overlooking the junction of the Grande Pierre valley and the valley of the River Cisse.

Ⓓ Viewpoint looking across fields of cereal crops and undulating meadowland.

Walk 12
PARC DE CHAMBORD

7 km (4¼ miles)   Easy

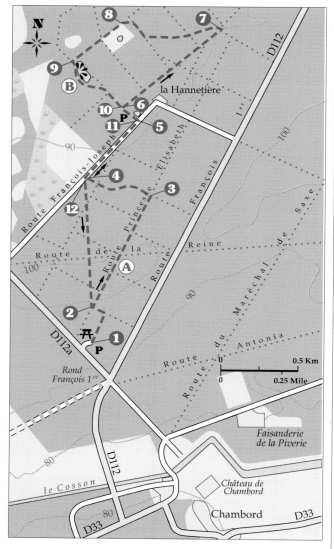

purpose. Even though you are unlikely to come across any wild boar, take heed of the warning near the entrance to the forest that *sangliers* live here!

The walk can be combined with a visit to the famous château, and tables near the car park at the start of the walk are ideal for a quiet picnic beneath the shade of the overhanging trees.

The 'wedding cake' Château de Chambord, the hunting lodge of King François I, was built in the 16th century, at about the same time as Hampton Court and St James's Palace. The château is the largest in the Loire Valley, allegedly built to a design created by Leonardo da Vinci. The extravagant structure is 156m by 117m (512ft by 384ft) and is linked by six massive towers. It has 440 public rooms, 14 main and 70 servants' staircases, and 365 fireplaces, each with its own separate chimney. Of all the architectural wonders of Chambord's château, the most famous is the double-spiral staircase between the main ante-rooms. A walkway around the building gives panoramic views of the park.

King François died before the building was complete. However, later kings, in particular Louis XIV, used it to entertain visiting royalty in lavish style, and Molière performed *Le Bourgeois Gentilhomme* at Chambord. A large part of French history is recalled in the furnishings of Chambord, especially its paintings and tapestries. Louis XV was the last true royal

The Château de Chambord is surrounded by 5,342 hectares of forest and parkland abounding in wildlife. To protect this fragile environment, access is restricted to a comparatively small area to the north of the château. The walk is through the accessible part of the forest and follows a waymarked route provided for that resident; the last private owner was the Comte de Chambord, who was the last of the line of Bourbon Pretenders to the throne of France. Since 1930, the château and its surrounding forests and parks have been designated a national monument, owned by the state.

If the prospect of walking round such a vast edifice is overwhelming, an alternative is to walk round the gardens, from which the size and grandure of Chambord can be appreciated.

The first *son-et-lumière* entertainments were staged at Chambord in the 1950s and continue nightly throughout the summer. Check performance times at a nearby tourist office.

While it is possible to buy a meal in one of the restaurants adjacent to the château, a picnic near the start of the walk might be preferable.

How to get there: The Château de Chambord is at the junction of the D112 Mer to Bracieux road and the D33 Blois to Thoury road. To reach the start of the walk, follow the D112 away from the château and in the direction of Mer, as far as the traffic island, the Rond-François 1er, then turn left onto the D112a, St. Dye-sur-Loire road. The car park by the start of the walk is along the second turning on the right, 400 metres down the road.

Route description

1 Follow stag's head waymarks diagonally left into the forest from the car park, then go left along a fire break.

2 Turn 90° right, along the arrow-straight forest ride. Go past three side openings on your left and two to your right.

3 Following the stag's head waymarks, turn left along a path curving beneath the trees.

4 Go to the right on reaching the forest access road, Route François Joseph.

5 Turn left into a car park beside a small pond, then out by way of a woodland footpath.

6 Go to the right, following waymarks along the forest track. Ignore side openings at right angles to your track.

7 On reaching another forest road, turn sharp left away from it and, still following the waymarks, walk along the forest path. Cross a fire break, turn right along the next break for 150 metres, then bear left to leave it, as indicated by waymarks.

8 Turn left along a wider track, past an open field with a small pond in its centre.

9 Turn left at a T-junction and follow a path around a reedy pool, then go ahead past two turnings on the right and left.

10 Follow the outward track past the small pool and into a car park.

11 Go to the right along the forest road.

12 Turn left from the road onto the furthest path (not the one followed on the outward leg of the walk) and follow it back to the car park at the start of the walk.

Points of interest

A A number of forest drives are named after past European royalty.

B Viewpoint overlooking the reed-lined pond. A hide on the opposite side of the pond is used for game-watching.

Walk 13
FORET DOM DE BOULOGNE

6 km (3¾ miles)   Easy

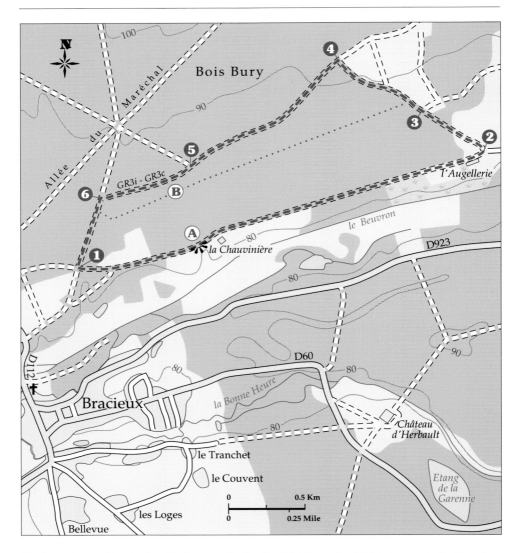

The forest has nothing to do with the town by the English Channel, which is known to the French as la Manche. It is part of the southern limits of the forest surrounding the Château de Chambord.

The district in which the forest lies is called the Sologne. A little visited area, it covers about a million hectares of forest, heath and tiny ponds. Many of the ponds were created as far back as Roman times, but most date from the Middle Ages when monks began to drain marshland. Country lanes used only by local traffic, and alive to the sound of birdsong, are ideal for gentle strolling. The walk begins by following one of these lanes above the northern bank of the Beuvron, one of the Loire tributaries that drains ponds (*étangs*) to the east.

Bracieux is the nearest place of any note. A small market town on the northern edge of the Sologne, it fills a clearing in the forest made by the junction of the Beuvron and a minor river from the south, the delightfully named Bonne Heure. The D112 crosses both rivers by attractive bridges, although the one over the Beuvron is the prettiest. There is a wide boulevard instead of a market square and the 16th-century covered market is inside a half-timbered tithe barn. Small, mostly privately owned châteaux line the valleys on either side of Bracieux.

Being a market town, Bracieux has a good range of restaurants and shops.

How to get there: The walk starts a little to the north of Bracieux. Follow the D112 across the River Beuvron for 250 metres, as far as a traffic island where the D923, Mont-près-Chambord road, turns left. Turn right at the traffic island, along an unsurfaced country road along the valley in the direction of Neuvy. Follow this track for 630 metres until it makes a sharp right-hand turn at a four-way junction. Park on the verge at the roadside.

Route description

1 Follow the main track around the bend to the right, between forest and open fields and along the valley for 2.75 km (almost 1³/₄ miles).

2 Go past a red-roofed cottage on your right and turn sharp left, then go gently uphill, following a rough track beside the forest edge on your left. Go through a short section of woodland then into the open scrubland and fields once again.

3 Still keeping the forest on your left, walk on past two tracks leaving to the right and head towards a dense line of pine trees.

4 Turn left at the track junction and follow white/red waymarks along the forest drive.

5 Bear left, following the waymarks at the track junction.

6 Turn left at the junction and continue ahead past the next junction, following the forest drive back to the valley road where you parked.

Points of interest

A Viewpoint across the woodland shrouded River Beuvron and towards the pleasant old market town of Bracieux.

B White/red waymarks indicate that this part of the walk follows a *Grande Randonnée*, a long distance walking route.

Walk 14
CHATEAU DE BEAUREGARD

5 km (3 miles)   Easy

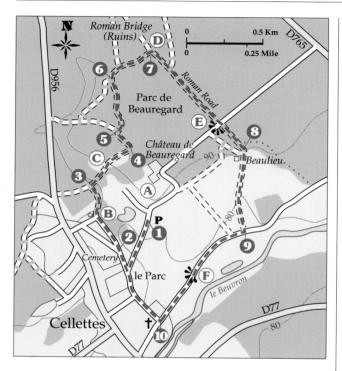

Châteaux built in the 17th century are smaller and slightly less formal than those built earlier, such as Chambord and Blois. Beauregard dates from this later period. Set in attractive informal parkland, it has more in common with the ideal of the English stately home. Gone is the need for military defence and the classical influence is more pronounced; gardens are less severe and water is used as an aesthetic feature, rather than for protection. Seventeenth-century châteaux have their English equivalents in Audley End and Hatfield House. The Court had moved back to Paris, so the need for lavish entertainment declined.

This walk begins from the Château de Beauregard on the outskirts of Cellettes and follows the boundary wall of parkland surrounding the château. It then enters the forest and returns to open farmland by way of a Roman road.

Cellettes is a quiet little town astride the D956, the road linking Contres and Blois. The latter is the regional capital for this part of the Loire Valley and makes an excellent base for anyone visiting the central part of the Loire. The old town is built around a 15th-century château perched on a hill above the river. Narrow streets and alleys wind towards the dominant castle, and are mostly traffic free.

Until Louis XIV, the 'Sun King', moved the court to Versailles, the fragmented nation was ruled from Blois. It was the seat of the Counts of Blois, rivals of the Counts of Anjou, and for centuries was at the centre of national events. However, when Louis moved out, Blois went into decline.

Extended by many of its owners from the 13th to 16th century, Blois' château is an unwieldy mixture of styles. The most interesting exterior feature is the ornate François I staircase which winds up four storeys to the roof. Inside there are two outstanding fireplaces and the emblems of royal residents. Catherine de Medici lived here and, in keeping with the scheming character of the Medici family, you can see the secret chamber next to her panelled dressing room, as well as the room where the Duc de Guise was assassinated in 1588. The son-et-lumière 'Esprits Aiment la Nuit' is staged at the château in Blois from April to September. There are some fine views of the older part of Blois from the far side of the Place du Château, and of the Loire beyond its attractive shaded gardens.

Cellettes has a couple of unpretentious little bars/restaurants, as well as food shops. For anything more, Blois is the obvious place to head for after the walk.

How to get there: Cellettes is reached by the D956, going south from Blois towards Cheverny. Follow the sign to the Château de Beauregard. There is a car park outside the entrance to the château.

Route description

1 Walk back towards the town, along the access lane from the château, and turn right along the side road, past the cemetery.

2 Take the right fork beyond the cemetery wall to walk along a side lane to the left of the park wall. Where the lane turns left go forwards and slightly uphill along a rough track.

3 Turn right and follow a forest track, still beside the boundary wall. Cross a shallow depression.

4 Go to the left opposite the old park gates, and walk on into the forest.

5 Bear right at the fork in the tracks, still in mature forest.

6 Swing to the right where another track joins from the left, and walk beside the park boundary wall. Ignore another track on the left (after about 60 metres).

7 Turn right at the track junction and follow the straight forest drive past side tracks to the left and across a wide forest ride.

8 Bear right with the main track and go past a ruined cottage, then downhill out of the forest and across open fields.

9 Turn right on reaching the road, following it back to Cellettes.

10 Turn right at the road junction next to the church. Follow the lane around the outskirts of the town and back to the château car park.

Points of interest

A Set in English-style parkland, the elegant Château de Beauregard once belonged to King François I, as well as to other notable ruling families. Jean de Thiers, minister under Henri II and associate of Ronsard, lived here. The floor of the Grand Gallery is paved with priceless Delftware tiles, and portraits of 363 16th-century nobles line its panelled walls. Examples of furniture and cabinet work date from the time of Henri II, and many of the exceptional decorations have remained unchanged since the 16th/17th century. The well-equipped 16th-century kitchen is especially worth seeing.

The Château de Beauregard is open all year round, but is closed Wednesdays from early February to March and October to January. Lunchtime closing is between 12.00 and 14.00. Guided visits take 30 minutes and there are pamphlets in English describing the chateau's features.

B The beehive-shaped well on the left once provided water for this part of Celletttes.

C Look over the wall on the left. The old kitchen garden is gradually being restored to its former glory.

D The track follows the line of a Roman road. A little over 120 metres to the left along the track is a tiny bridge which is reputed to be Roman. This is worth a short diversion.

E Viewpoint. The elegant château set amidst wooded parkland, stands at the head of a long forest drive.

F Viewpoint across fields and vineyards lining the Beuvron, and towards Cellette, with its church spire beckoning in the middle distance.

Walk 15
THE PONDS OF COURMEMIN   6 km (3¾ miles)   Easy

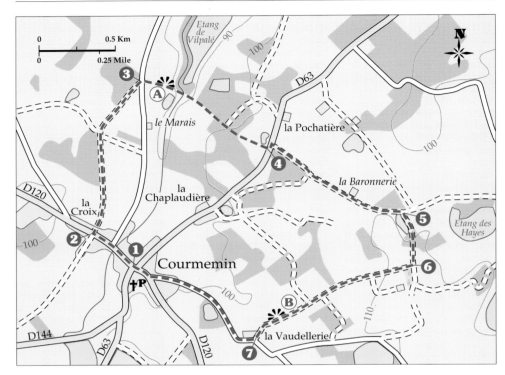

The heaths and woodlands of the Sologne are dotted with thousands of ponds (*étangs*). Most are man-made, and many of them date from the time when the Romans (or later, Medieval monks) drained what was then a malarial swamp. Today the ponds contain water drained off the surrounding land, saving it for irrigation in dry periods. They also contain fish, thereby drawing local anglers, and because of their age, the ponds have become wildlife havens – home to water voles, beavers and birdlife, including kingfishers with electric blue plumage.

Intensively farmed in Roman times, by the Middle Ages the Sologne had reverted to a vast impenetrable forest containing dangerous swamps. Even the Hundred Years War and the upheavals of the Revolution had little impact on this impoverished region. Continuing work begun by the monasteries as long ago as the 11th century, in the 19th century local landowners improved the system of meres which are now the main feature of the Sologne landscape.

Sologne's architecture is unique, reflecting the slow reform of agriculture in the last century. The oldest dwellings are single-storeyed, built with timber frames in-filled with a mixture of clay and straw, called cob. They were superseded by more low timber-framed structures, but with herring-bone brick patterns in place of cob. Both of these types of buildings are still to be found in the Sologne, particularly in Courmemin where this walk begins and ends. The village is typical of this part of the Loire region, a simple cluster of buildings around a crossroads. You will still find the traditional baker's shop alongside a small butcher's shop and general store, together with a couple of friendly local bars with a similar atmosphere to traditional English pubs.

Romorantin-Lanthenay is to the south-east of Courmemin, along the D120. The 'capital' of Sologne, it lies on the banks of the River Sauldre. Although the modern town is a sprawl of unattractive developments, the central and oldest part of Romorantin is a delightful mix of half-timbered buildings and 19th-century town houses and shops. The Musée de Sologne in the Town Hall covers the development of the region and includes the traditional interiors of two cottages. Matra racing cars are made in Romorantin and you can see an exhibition of them at the Musée Municipal de la Course Automobile at 29-32 Faubourg d'Orléans.

Chez Micheline in Courmemin is a small half-timbered bar/restaurant where you can buy a simple meal in friendly surroundings. Otherwise the *boulangerie* around the corner will have everything you need to make up a picnic.

How to get there: Take the D765 Blois to Romorantin-Lanthenay road as far as la Troanne, then the D144 to Courmemin. Alternatively, follow the D120 north-west from Romorantin. Park near the church in the centre of the village.

Route description

1 From the staggered crossroads in the centre of Courmemin, follow the D120 north-westwards in the direction of Fontaines-en-Sologne. Go past a side road to your right and walk on to where a rough track crosses the main road.

2 Turn right along the unsurfaced track, following it between fields where melons or artichokes are often grown, then beside a small wood. Go over crosstracks and skirt another small wood.

3 Cross the surfaced road to follow a raised narrow grassy track into ancient woodland. Go over a little footbridge, then walk uphill through a patch of woodland and beside small fields.

4 Cross the main road to follow the track opposite, signposted to the farm of la Baronnerie. Walk on past a wood and a track joining from the right, then past the farm. Follow the track alongside a wood as far as a small pond on your right.

5 Turn right to walk beside the pond and through a wood on its far side. Beyond the wood, cross a field and walk towards a small vineyard.

6 Go to the right at a track junction, skirting a vineyard, and on between fields, then over a slight rise. Go past two side turnings on the left, and one on the right, into the farm settlement of la Vaudellerie.

7 Turn right along the country lane, following it back into Courmemin.

Points of interest

A Viewpoint. The tree-shaded pond is a favourite fishing place not only for human anglers, but for kingfishers too.

B Viewpoint. Ahead is the sleepy, mostly half-timbered village of Courmemin. It is typical of Sologne villages whose prosperity came after the surrounding swamps were finally drained in the early 19th century.

Walk 16
ST. AIGNAN

6.5 km (4 miles)   Easy/Moderate

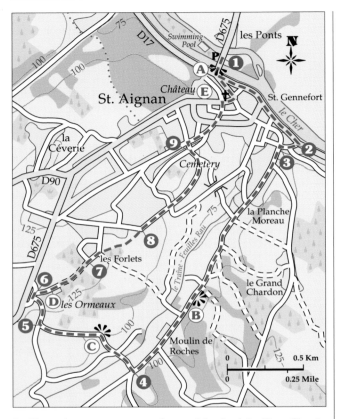

St. Aignan is a pretty town on the south bank of the River Cher in the Touraine region. Best viewed from across the river, the old town is dominated by a massive but largely abandoned château fortress. Medieval streets wind their way to the hilltop château, which is only accessible via a series of wide steps. The castle is not open to the public except by special permission, but the climb is worthwhile if only to admire the view from a terrace beneath the mouldering ramparts. Half-timbered houses with plaster infilling lean at crazy angles over the narrow streets. The church is early Gothic with a crypt decorated with frescoes painted between 1100 and 1500. The oldest and most magnificent of these is entitled *Christ in Majesty*. The D675 leads north from St. Aignan, through the Forêt de Gros Bois, to St. Romain-sur-Cher, where a minor road on the right winds its way through vineyards and pleasant woodland to the stately Manoir de Beauregard. Going south from the town, the great swathe of the Forêt de Brouard is broken by the

D675. Also along this road, 4 km (2½ miles) south of the town, is the *Parc Ornithologique de Beauval*, a bird sanctuary concentrating on endangered species. The sanctuary is open daily until nightfall.

The walk starts beside the river Cher, by a bridge which links an island and its *piscine* (swimming pool) with both shores. The road along the valley floor, the D17, follows the river upstream beyond the outskirts of the town. From here the walk follows the side valley of the Traîne-Feuilles tributary, out of the town and past attractive groups of modern and old houses. Farm lanes climb out of the valley, past ancient properties and farmsteads to the vineyards of les Ormeaux, home of the *Appellation Contrôlée Earl Thomas*. Skirting modern developments, the walk returns to St. Aignan along ancient backstreets below the ruined château.

St. Aignan has a number of moderately priced restaurants, mostly along the side streets below the château. There is also a supermarket in the main square above the oldest part of the town. A short distance to the north-east of St. Aignan there is a riverside campsite.

Red/white waymarking and signposts indicate that the GR41, Cher Valley *Grande Randonnée*, long distance walking route, passes through St. Aignan.

How to get there: St. Aignan is at the crossing of the D675 Contres to Châtillon-sur-Indre road and the D17 Selles-sur-Cher to Bleré road. The N76 also follows the Cher valley west from the A71 autoroute, which runs south from Orléans. Leave the N76 at La Croix Verte, across the river from St. Aignan. Park on the island in the middle of the River Cher, close to the swimming pool below the town.

Route description

1 Cross the bridge in the direction of St. Aignan and turn left along the D17, following the road upstream.

2 Look for the road sign marking the outskirts of St. Aignan and turn right by the sign, onto a side lane. Walk up the lane past another side lane on the left and as far as a minor crossroads.

3 Turn left along the quiet valley road signposted to Nouans. Walk past a mixture of old and new houses, all with pleasant gardens. Move out between fields and woodland and towards open country, continuing for just under 2 km (1¼ miles).

4 Go to the right at a staggered crossroads, then over the stream and ahead at the next crossroads. Climb to the left past a highly photogenic and venerable farmhouse.

5 Turn right at the T-junction to continue uphill along the lane and towards a vineyard.

6 Go hard right at the staggered crossroads (signposted for the Earl Thomas vineyards). Go past les Ormeaux farm on your right, then along the track between vines. Begin to go downhill towards a modern housing estate.

7 Join a road and follow it for a short way past the houses. Where the road starts to bear left, continue ahead along a grassy path downhill, past a vineyard and through open fields.

8 Go forwards where the path rejoins the road. Follow the road until it forks (signposted right to Tours and Blois). Continue ahead, then bear left and go along this urban road past the cemetery and towards the centre of St. Aignan.

9 Go over the crossroads marked by a traffic island and turn right at either of the next two roads to go downhill through the old town and towards the river and bridge to the island where you started.

Points of interest

A Viewpoint. There is a good view of the old town and its abandoned château from the bridge. The river was once navigable and the weir beneath the bridge kept the water level high enough to work canal locks here and upstream.

B The Domaine des Roches, whose vineyards line the skyline on the left, proudly advertises that its wines are classified by the *Appellation Contrôlée Vins de Touraine.*

C Viewpoint looking along the tranquil upper valley of the Traîne-Feuilles.

D The vineyards of Earl Thomas are *Appellation Controlée Vins de Touraine et Gamay.* Wine-tasting (*dégustation*) is available.

E St. Aignan. The venerable keep of the mouldering château overlooks the old town. Steps leading to the castle terrace go past the early Gothic church. Narrow winding streets in the town centre are lined with medieval half-timbered properties. Look out for the dusty looking 'bric-a-brac' (*brocante*) shop in the leaning building on the corner of a side street at a tangent to the main street. This is a good place to browse for unrecognised antiques.

A pretty water garden at the head of the main street is a cool resting place on a hot day. A fountain fed by an underground stream trickles through an arbour built from tufa, and pools in the centres of the flower beds are filled with lively trout and golden carp.

Walk 17
CHATEAU DE GUE-PEAN

4 km (2½ miles)   Easy/Moderate

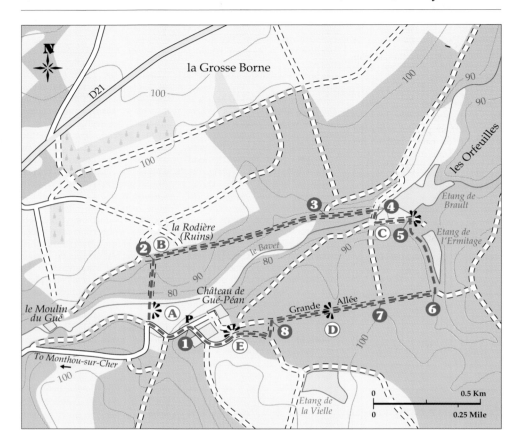

The Château of Gué-Péan could not be more romantic. Its woodland setting complements its four-square, Scots-baronial appearance. Hidden at the end of a long broad-leaved woodland drive, the château contrasts markedly with the opulent grandeur of Ambois or Chambord to its north. While life at the grand châteaux would have centred around the artificial round of court protocol, one can imagine that living at Gué-Péan would have been much more peaceful.

Complementing a visit to the château, the walk follows tracks and woodland paths around the forested grounds and parkland surrounding the house, and past two tree-shaded man-made lakes which once powered the local water mill.

There are several suitable picnic sites beneath the overhanging branches of massive horse chestnut trees. Otherwise, Monthou-sur-Cher, 2 km (1¼ miles) along the valley below the château, has a number of small but good restaurants.

How to get there: Access is signposted from the main road, the N76 between Selles-sur-Cher and Montrichard. Turn north-east along the D21 for 2 km (1¼ miles) to Monthou-sur-Cher, then turn right to follow the minor lane signposted to the Château de Gué-Péan. Park next to the château entrance.

If approaching from the east along the N76, look out at Thésée for the substantial roadside ruins of a Roman granary.

Route description

1 Walk back from the château beneath the avenue of horse chestnut trees as far as the ruined farmhouse above the left-hand bend in the road. Following yellow waymarks, turn hard right along a grassy path crossing the open meadow below. Beyond the meadow, climb through woodland and follow a partly sunken track uphill.

2 On the far side of the wood, turn right at a track junction. The track initially follows the woodland edge, then it re-enters the forest and starts to go downhill.

3 Go forwards at a track junction above a forest clearing, and still in the forest, continue gently downhill until you join another track at a T-junction.

4 Turn right at the junction, past an old forest building then over a bridge. Immediately after the bridge, turn left and follow the stream towards a dam.

5 Continue about 25 metres past a fork in the track, then turn right onto a woodland path beside a narrow reservoir, the Etang de l'Ermitage. Walk to the far end of the reservoir.

6 Turn right on joining a forest track.

7 Go forwards on joining another improving forest track, downhill at first then up between an avenue of tall trees.

8 Turn left then right with the track (do not go towards the château) and continue along the steadily improving track. Bear right with the track to reach the château.

Points of interest

A Viewpoint. The Château de Gué-Péan is open daily throughout the year. Visits take about 45 minutes and there is a commentary in English. Note the curious bell-shaped roof of the nearest tower. The ruined building above the bend in the drive was once a farmhouse associated with the château. Horse chestnut trees (at their best in late spring) make an attractive foil for the view of the château from the lower meadow.

B The ruined farmhouse of la Rodière was once one of the château's properties. Its lands are now swallowed up in larger concerns, or covered by forest.

C Viewpoint. The reservoirs of the Etangs Brault and l'Ermitage once provided water to drive the now abandoned Moulin du Gué lower down the valley.

D Viewpoint looking along the tree-lined avenue towards the château's rooftops.

E Viewpoint over the surrounding outer wall towards the southern aspect of the house.

Walk 18
CHAUMONT-SUR-LOIRE   6 km (3¾ miles)   Easy/Moderate

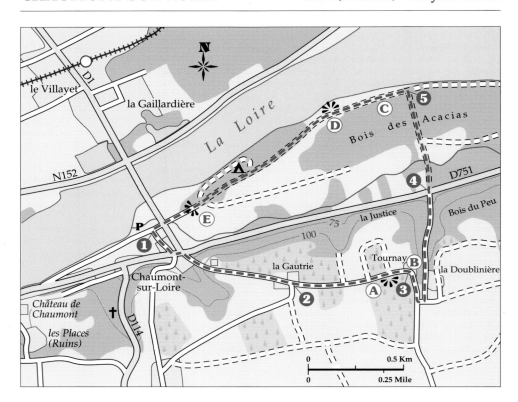

Here is a short walk around rich farmland and vineyards surrounding the 'home' village of the 15th-century Château de Chaumont. A woodland stroll along the riverside complements the farming oriented early part of the walk.

The walk is an ideal accompaniment to a visit to the château, or it could be an evening stroll for anyone staying at the riverside campsite in the Bois des Acacias. Hydrofoil riverboat cruises leave the landing stage below the château.

Chaumont was built in the 15th century, at about the same time as the châteaux of Blois and Gien, and Hever and Herstmonceaux in England. Its style is heavily influenced by the use of gunpowder and cannons in post-medieval warfare, which had a drastic effect on the design of castles from the 15th century onwards. Thick walls and arrow slits were no longer an effective defence against attackers; walls needed to be secure not only against cannon balls, but also undermining. As a result castles built in the 15th century tend to have much stronger walls and rounded towers to withstand the impact of bombarding cannon balls. The design of defence systems of barbicans, inner and outer wards and gun ports became a complex art. Despite its military aspect, some thought was given to creature comfort at Chaumont, and many of the more important rooms are quite palatial.

The Château de Chaumont is open daily from January to December. Guided visits lasting 30 minutes include the stables and park. Only the park can be visited without a guide.

There are a number of restaurants along the riverside, on the main street at the foot of the castle. The Bois des Acacias and riverside locations downstream of the bridge both offer ideal sites for impromptu picnics.

How to get there: Access to Chaumont-sur-Loire is either from the D751 Blois to Amboise road by way of the Beuvron valley, or from the N152 by following the north bank of the Loire, again between Blois and Amboise. If using the N152, cross the Loire by the bridge which links Onzain and Chaumont-sur-Loire. Park at the riverside immediately downstream of the bridge.

Route description

❶ Follow the side road away from the river and cross the main road, going diagonally left across the road from the bridge. Take care crossing the main road at this point as it is at the junction of three busy routes. Go between a set of bollards and take the narrow pedestrianised road steeply uphill through woodland. At the top of the rise and where the gradient eases, walk between a vineyard and small fields, passing pretty gardens fronting interesting farmhouses and cottages.

❷ Move ahead at the junction and follow the lane past further vineyards and fields growing high value crops such as melons and globe artichokes.

❸ Follow the lane to the right and begin to go downhill to a road junction. Turn sharp left at the junction to go steeply downhill, past a farm and down a narrow valley.

❹ Cross the main road and follow the partly raised track along the woodland edge on the right of a field. Go through a narrow belt of trees, then across an open field system. Continue forwards where another track leaves to the right, and go through a wider stretch of woodland.

❺ Turn left at the junction and follow the grassy track, with plantation woodland on your left and scrub woodland masking the River Loire to your right. Continue along this track, in and out of trees and past allotment gardens and the campsite, back to the bridge.

Points of interest

Ⓐ Cereals, as well as high value crops and vines, are grown in the surrounding fields. Over to your right you should get a glimpse of the sturdy rooftops of Chaumont castle.

Ⓑ The old well once provided drinking water for nearby farms on this rapidly draining hillside. Despite the heat, do not drink the water as modern farming methods may have polluted it.

Ⓒ The aptly named Bois des Acacias is composed mainly of these African trees.

Ⓓ Viewpoint with tempting glimpses of the Loire's shady river bank.

Ⓔ Viewpoint. Tantalisingly, only part of the château's once formidable ramparts are visible. This is the only viewpoint on the approach to the bridge.

Walk 19
GRAND ETANG DE JUMEAUX

4 km (2½ miles)   Easy

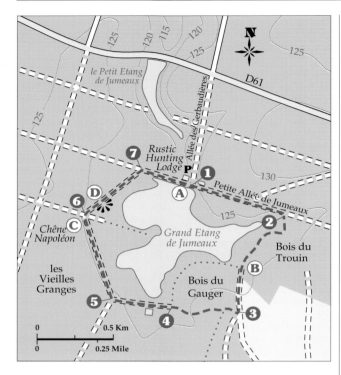

14-year-old Louis d'Orléans. England's Richard Coeur-de-Lion was imprisoned at the behest of Emperor Henri VI in a tiny cell in nearby Montrichard castle. Montrichard has a delightful riverside park with a swimming pool.

Close to Montrichard is Nanteuil, where there is a 12th-century church containing some interesting carvings of human faces and a two-storey chapel, the Lady Chapel, which was built by Louis XI.

This woodland stroll takes little more than an hour and a half to complete, so unless you plan to explore the forest around lunchtime, it will not be necessary to carry anything other than a drink and perhaps a small snack. Restaurants may be found at Amboise and Montrichard, on the River Cher.

How to get there: Follow the D61 Montrichard road for 9 km (5½ miles) south-east from Amboise to reach the start of the walk. The woodland turning is hard to find, but on entering the forest from the north, look out for the last of three woodland reservoirs on the right as you drive across their dams. A little under 300 metres beyond the last reservoir, and opposite a lane signposted to Souvigny-de-Touraine, turn right along an unsurfaced forest drive. If the barrier is down, park at the side of the track (it will then be necessary to walk nearly 1 km (half a mile) along the drive to reach the start of the walk); otherwise drive on to the junction with another track next to the Etang de Jumeaux and park beside the rustic hunting lodge.

The subject of this walk is a partially hidden man-made lake deep inside the Forêt d'Amboise, about 9 km (5½ miles) south-east of Amboise town. The forest was the ancient hunting ground of the Dukes of Choiseul who once owned the château overlooking Amboise. Any peasant caught stealing game from the Duke's property to feed his family would have been severely punished. Today this semi-natural forest is carefully managed to provide substantial timber reserves for saw mills in the locality. Divided into sections both for easy access and to create fire breaks, many of the ancient forest rides are named after local nobles.

Do not be put off by the *privée* (private) notice near the entrance to the drive leading to the start of this walk. It refers to hunting rights only, and provided you walk without disturbing game and do not light fires, no-one should object to you walking in the forest.

Montrichard and Amboise are roughly equidistant from the *étang*. A fortress-like ruined château in Amboise overlooks a cluster of grey-roofed houses and a sturdy church. The church is where the hunch-backed and facially deformed 12-year-old Jeanne-de-France, daughter of Louis XI, entered into an arranged marriage with

Route description

1 Facing the lake, turn left and follow the forest drive. Go past a turning on the left and walk on for another 300 metres.

2 Turn right along a narrow woodland path winding its way well back from, but roughly paralleling the reservoir's shore-line. Where the path enters an open field, walk with the forest boundary on your right, along a wider track.

3 Beyond a narrow enclosure on your left, look for a narrow track turning right. Go down it for about 10 metres, then where it turns left, walk on along a narrow forest path. Begin to go slightly downhill beneath the shelter of mature trees.

4 Follow a raised track across marshy ground.

5 Turn right along a wide forest track.

6 Go to the right on joining the forest road, and follow it around the lake.

7 At the junction with a rough track, keep to the right with the wider lane and follow it back to the forest hunting lodge.

Points of interest

A The rustic lodge overlooks the reedy lake, the Grand Etang de Jumeaux. This is a popular venue for weekend fishermen.

B In the tranquil silence of the forest you may see roe deer, wild boar and red squirrels, and hear the songs of woodland birds.

C *Chêne Napoléon*. The massive oak is dedicated to the Emperor of France who tried unsuccessfully to unify Europe.

D Viewpoint overlooking the now naturalised man-made lake.

Walk 20
PAGODA DE CHANTELOUP

3 km (1¾ miles)
Easy (suitable for wheelchairs)

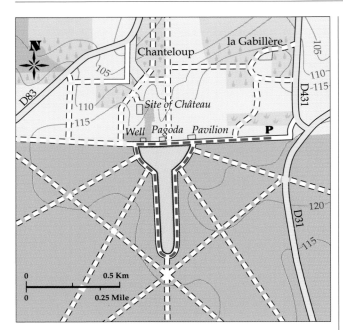

All that is left of the Château de Chanteloup is a Chinese-style pagoda. This slender tower was once the central feature of a large and formal pleasure garden. The château stood to the north of the pagoda, overlooking Amboise, but following its abandonment and pillage during the Reign of Terror after the Revolution, the building became untenable. The once opulent mansion was finally destroyed in 1823 and all that remains are a few outbuildings and grassy mounds over the rubble of the main building.

Tea drinking became fashionable in the late 18th century, and with it an interest in Chinese architecture and decorations. The Duke of Choiseul, owner of Chanteloup and a Minister at Louis XV's Court, disgraced himself and had to leave Versailles. He subsequently retired to Chanteloup, and in gratitude for the fidelity of his friends he directed his architect, Le Camus, to design and build the pagoda in 1775. The resulting structure combines 18th-century French design with the architect's interpretation of a Chinese pagoda.

Immediately popular with pleasure seeking courtiers, the pagoda became the focal point of the social life of the château. It over-looked a formal lake and the ground floor could accommodate fairly large gatherings where the socialites took tea and indulged in polite chatter or political scheming. Stone staircases starting as a wide sweep lead to ever narrowing upper chambers and airy balconies with views of the distant Loire, and the town and château of Amboise. In keeping with the true pagoda, the design encourages updraughts to keep the interior cool on hot days.

The 44-metre high pagoda, along with two other interesting relics of the formerly grand garden, is maintained by a voluntary association, the Friends of Chanteloup. The other relics are an ornate well-head to the west of a dam holding back the pond, where horses pulling coaches from the château could be watered; and on the opposite side of the pond from the pagoda, a small domed pavilion in which old plans, engravings and paintings showing the splendour of the Château de Chanteloup are now exhibited. At one time the pagoda was in danger of collapse (and indeed it still leans a little), but in 1910 the architect René-Edouard André set about its restoration. Since then the Friends of Chanteloup (*l'Association des Amis de Chanteloup*) have taken on the responsibility for its upkeep.

The walk can be combined with a visit to nearby Amboise. This busy town clusters at the foot of its 16th-century Renaissance château. Part of the town centre is pedestrianised, which makes it a pleasant place to explore. Amboise developed beside the Loire from the Roman town of *Ambacia*. Caves below the hill on which the château stands are reputed to have been used as granaries since the time of the Roman occupation. In AD 503, a treaty was arranged at

Amboise between Clovis, leader of the Franks, and Alaric II, king of the Visigoths. Later, during raids along the river valleys of France, Vikings attacked Amboise and murdered most of the population. Centuries later, the young Mary Queen of Scots lived at Amboise when she was married to François II.

The château which overlooks Amboise developed its stately grandure in the early part of the 16th century. Many features of its design show Italian influence, and particularly that of Leonardo da Vinci, who spent the last four years of his life nearby at Clos-Lucé and was a frequent visitor at the château. A collection of models built from his amazing inventions – including the first aeroplane, the first self-propelled vehicle, the helicopter, the parachute, the machine gun and the swing bridge – are on display at Clos-Lucé near the main château. Da Vinci's bedroom, kitchen and other rooms have been carefully restored to their Renaissance splendour by the French Beaux-Arts Department, together with the beautiful Italianate Rose Garden. A stream flows through the park, past the jewel-like chapel built by Charles VIII for his wife, Anne of Brittany.

The château at Amboise hosts a *son-et-lumière* performance, *Soirée à la Cour du Roy*, and stages a Renaisssance party with 420 performers, including dancers, riders and jugglers in period costume. Performances start at 22.00 and are held on advertised evenings from the end of June to the end of August. Concerts, wine fairs and Sunday morning markets also take place in Amboise.

How to get there: The Pagoda de Chanteloup is signposted from the D431 near its junction with the D31 beyond the southern outskirts of Amboise. Park at the end of the drive.

Route description
The walk simply follows the drive from the entrance kiosk up to the pagoda, and continues around the old pond, passing the pavilion and information centre along the way. The views from the top of the pagoda are not to be missed, but anyone who suffers from vertigo might find the balconies a little too narrow.

As the path is firm and level all the way, the walk is easily accessible for pushchairs and invalid carriages.

It is posible to buy a made-up picnic basket on site, but visitors may prefer to take their own. Either way, the park beyond the pond offers ideal picnic sites from which you can view the pagoda and watch the antics of water-fowl.

Walk 21
BEAUMONT-LA-RONCE

5 km (3 miles)   Easy/Moderate

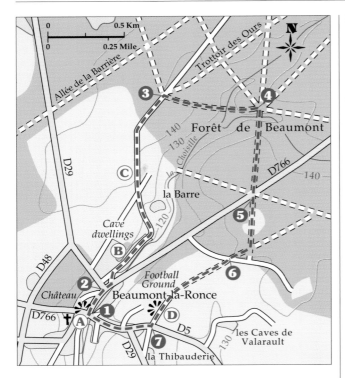

Surrounded by modern housing and industrial development, the approach into Tours leaves much to be desired. However, the city's medieval heart, centred on the Place Jean Jaurès, is unspoilt. Many of its narrow streets, lined with half-timbered tall buildings, are traffic free. Ancient buildings, some of them incorporating fragments dating from the Gallo-Roman period (such as the cathedral), are a blend of Renaissance and Gothic styles. Tours is rich in museums and has a colourful market.

One of the loveliest and therefore most popular of Loire châteaux, Chenonceau, sits on a romantic bridge across the River Cher to the south-east of Tours. Built on the site of a mill 400 years ago by Thomas Bohier, Chamberlain to four kings, its formal gardens, grounds and magnificent rooms are open to the public. A *son-et-lumière*, entitled *Aux Temps des Dames de Chenonceau*, emphasises the part women have played in the château's history.

The forest to the north-east of Beaumont-la-Ronce, the Forêt de Beaumont, is used for hunting between November and March, so anyone attempting this walk during that period should keep a sharp lookout for light-fingered huntsmen. Mushroom picking is carefully controlled and and it is essential to obtain permission if you wish to gather these delicacies. With the above provisos, the locals welcome walkers in this little known corner of the Loire Valley.

Beaumont-la-Ronce is one of those small towns off the beaten track, where time seems to stand still. It is a place to search for hidden by-ways and unexpected views. Diligent explorers will discover a row of caves on the outskirts of the town, where in living memory families made their homes.

Although this walk is extremely rural, it is only 20 km (12 miles) north of Tours. The city is an ideal base for anyone who wants to combine the advantages of the diversions it has to offer with ease of access to countryside on either side of the Loire.

Tours' importance dates from the 4th century, when pilgrims came to worship at the miraculous shrine of St. Martin. The city's reputation increased when Gregory of Tours founded its monastic college. Charlemagne forged long-standing links with the English church when he invited Alcuin of York to become its abbot. Almost constant warfare and invasions throughout the Middle Ages caused the city's fortunes to rise and fall, but greater stability benefited Tours in the 15th and 16th centuries. It was during this time that the art of silk weaving developed there, an art that is still practiced in Tours.

There are a few small bars/restaurants where the food, though unpretentious, is excellent value, and where the locals will welcome tourists. Alternatively, the *boulangeries*, *pâtisseries* and *charcuteries* in the town centre will sell everything necessary for a picnic.

How to get there: Beaumont-la-Ronce is at the junction of the D766 Château-Renault to Neuillé-Pont-Pierre road, and the D29 Tours to la Chartre-sur-le-Loir road, about 20 km (12 miles) north of Tours. Park close to the church near the town centre.

Route description

1 From the church, follow the D766 in the direction of Château-Renault, alongside a high wall screening the garden of a small château.

2 Where the main road forks, continue ahead for 10 metres or so, then turn half left to follow a narrow side lane, the Rue de Carrières. Walk past a children's playpark, then past partly abandoned troglodyte houses. Begin to go uphill into farmland. Continue ahead at the crossroads.

3 Soon after entering woodland, turn right along a grassy forest track. Go gently downhill, then over a narrow stream. Climb to the junction of six forest tracks.

4 Turn sharp right at the track junction, going downhill again to cross another stream. Climb through the forest until you reach the main road. Cross with care.

5 Take the right-hand track of two adjacent forest tracks and go gently downhill. Cross a clearing then re-enter the forest and continue until you reach a track turning right. Go with this track towards an access drive along the forest edge.

6 Cross the drive and walk down a steadily improving lane, between fields and past the football ground. Bear left with the lane, ignoring path turn-offs on the right, until you reach a side road, the D5.

7 Turn right, then right again on joining the main D29. Follow this road downhill into the town centre of Beaumont-la-Ronce.

Points of interest

A Viewpoint. The attractive château on the left has a tall lookout tower which dates from less peaceful times, when it was necessary to be prepared for an unexpected attack.

B The long low sandstone cliff, at the side of the road on the left, is riddled with cave dwellings. The dry stone made the houses cool in summer and warm in winter. The only structural adjustments needed were to drill a hole through the ceiling for the chimney and brick up the entrance, leaving space for a door and windows. Generations of families lived this way, but nowadays few caves are inhabited and the former cave dwellings serve as storage places or garages.

C Many of the apple trees in the orchard to your right have been killed off by parasitic mistletoe.

D Viewpoint overlooking Beaumont-la-Ronce. The church fills the central space, but the château rises over both the church and town.

Walk 22
SEMBLANCAY

4 km (2½ miles)   Easy

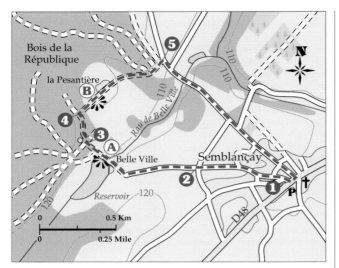

Route description

1 Go to the right from the square and follow the country lane behind the modern shops. Follow it out beyond the last houses and into open country.

2 Go over a crossroads, then along a rough track, past a reservoir and into shady woodland. Go forwards at a track junction above the reservoir.

3 Turn right at a T-junction, then almost immediately left to follow another woodland track past a small pond.

4 Turn sharp right at the track junction and climb slightly out of the forest and across open fields surrounding the group of farm buildings at la Pesantière.

5 Turn right on reaching the quiet side road. Follow it across a shallow valley, in and out of woodland, back to Semblançay.

Points of interest

A Viewpoint looking across the reedy shores of the reservoir, where ducks and visting birds abound on this naturalised stretch of water.

B Viewpoint looking over fields and small woods towards Semblançay and the distant Loire.

Driving on the long straight roads of central France can be tedious and it helps break the monotony if you can leave the road and take a little gentle exercise in pleasant surroundings. Not only will it be safer than driving whilst tired, but taking a short walk in relatively unknown territory can be a voyage of discovery.

This short, gentle stroll starts at a tiny village well away from the bustle of traffic, yet conveniently close to both the N138 Tours to le Mans road, and the D959 Tours to la Flèche road. Semblançay is a pleasant cluster of old and new houses surrounding an attractive church.

Château de Lude is in its namesake village on the D959 a little to the north-west of Semblançay. Lavish *son-et-lumières* take place in the grounds of the château. A group of modern shops conveniently near the start of the walk can provide everything for a woodland picnic. Alternatively, if the walk is timed right, lunch could be taken at the restaurant in the village square beside the church.

How to get there: Semblançay is on the D48 which links the N138 and D959, north-west of Tours. Park by the church in the central square.

Walk 23

THE ORCHARDS OF LIGNIERES-DE-TOURAINE

10 km (6¼ miles)   Easy/Moderate
(Suitable for push chairs)

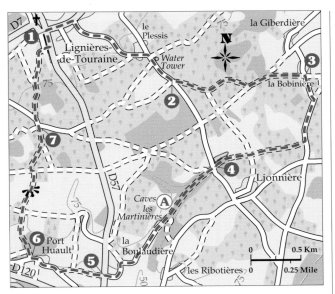

Fruit growing is the main industry in this part of Touraine. The walk follows tracks and back lanes through orchards growing apples, pears and cherries. Lignières sits astride a crossroads on the north-western corner of a group of hills between the Loire and Indre rivers.

The nearby château at Azay-le-Rideau is worth visiting. This pretty 16th-century building appears to float on an artificially created loop of the River Indre. It is now in the care of the state and the rooms are decorated with sumptuous Renaissance furnishings, tapestries and paintings. Every summer the château hosts a nightly *son-et-lumière*.

There is a handful of small shops and bar/restaurants on either side of the crossroads in and around Lignières-de-Touraine.

How to get there: From Tours, follow the D7 south-west along the Loire valley. Alternatively, the D57 between Langeais and Azay-le-Rideau goes through Lignières-de-Touraine. Park as close as you can to the centre of the village without interfering with other traffic.

Route description

1 Follow the Villandry road for 300 metres and turn right at the second lane on the right, the Rue des Colasdières. Go uphill through a grassy cutting to the hamlet of le Plessis. Turn right and go past a water tower and between orchards.

2 Turn left onto a fairly level gravel track between a series of orchards. Ignore minor side tracks. Turn left at the junction with a second track from the right. Bear slightly right and proceed into la Bobinière.

3 Turn right along the surfaced country lane, past further orchards, then turn right along a narrow track, past an abandoned house. Go downhill, over crosstracks and then past a small reservoir, to a side road.

4 Go diagonally right across the road, then turn left down a cart track, bearing left again at a track junction. Walk down the narrow wooded valley to the little château of les Martinières, where the track becomes a surfaced lane. Continue downhill to the main road, the D57.

5 Cross the road and follow the field track opposite. When it joins a side lane, go ahead through the hamlet of Port Huault, to a wood on the right.

6 Turn right, steeply uphill along a field track following the woodland edge. Go through the upper part of the wood then out into open fields. Go over the crosstracks and proceed steadily uphill. Bear left then immediately right at a staggered crosstracks. Turn half left at the junction with another track.

7 Turn left at a by-road, then right where the road swings left, downhill on a track between orchards and a small wood. Bear right beside a cemetery, then left on reaching the main road to return to the centre of Lignières.

Point of interest

A Man-made caves, carved out of the low sandstone cliff at the right-hand side of the track, once stored maturing local vintages.

Walk 24
VILLANDRY

5 km (3 miles)   Easy

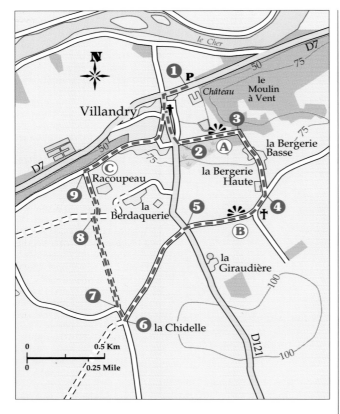

Whilst the historic interior of the château should not be missed, most visitors come to Villandry to view its extraordinary 16th-century garden. A large proportion of the complex beds are marked out by low box hedges, filled not with flowers, but vegetables!

The gardens have been constructed on three tiers, watered by fountains that are powered by a small lake on the highest level. On the lowest level, near the entrance, there is a kitchen garden (*jardin potager*), where herbs and vegetables are laid out in amazingly colourful designs. With few exceptions, almost every vegetable we eat today is used; the only common one missing is the potato, as it had not yet reached France in the 16th century. Each year different varieties of everyday vegetables are planted. Most of the beds have forget-me-nots and daisies as in-filling colour to augment the warm reds and greens of the vegetables.

Above the kitchen garden are the ornamental and herb gardens, where tall box and yew topiary has created the shapes of musical instruments. A canal separates the 'Musical Garden' from the 'Love Garden', where whole and broken hearts are often filled with dahlias. On the highest level, the ornamental pond which irrigates the gardens is home to stately swans and is surrounded by shady arbours created by clipped limes.

Terraces reached by steps and walkways overlook the gardens, giving not only a bird's eye impression of the complex layout, but also a broad view of the Loire as it flows past the château on its way to the sea. Rose beds alternate with those already described, contrasting brightly with the generally darker shades of herbs, vegetables and other flowers.

Villandry château was built in 1536 by Jean le Breton, Finance Minister to François I. It was the last great Renaissance château to go up on the Loire. Built in the classical 'cour d'honneur' horseshoe plan, the almost perfect acoustic qualities of its restored interior rooms makes Villandry an ideal venue for concerts.

The home village of Villandry is built around a shallow gully on the west side of the château. Often neglected by visitors who are only interested in the delights of the château, the village warrants more than a passing glance. A Norman-style church stands in the centre of the oldest part of Villandry, surrounded by houses in a variety of styles, many several centuries old. The narrow streets and tiny alleys appear to have been built randomly.

Quiet by-lanes reach out from Villandry into rolling farmland where for centuries families living in the village, if they did not work at the château, toiled in the lush and fertile fields.

The walk combines perfectly with a visit to the château and it provides a good excuse to explore the surrounding farmland. The best time to visit Villandry's château is in the morning, so let the walk give you an appetite for lunch at one of the restaurants adjacent to the château, or alongside the locals in one of the village hostelries.

How to get there: Villandry is south-west of Tours at the junction of the D121 cross-country road with the D7 Loire Valley road running from Tours towards Chinon. Park either by the château or in front of the church where it is usually less crowded.

Route description

❶ From the château, walk into the village and turn left, uphill along the street passing the church. Continue to a five-way junction on the edge of the village.

❷ Turn left along a side lane signposted to la Bergerie Basse, and go past the garden gates of the château.

❸ Go to the right with the surfaced lane, then uphill past old farmhouses and between meadows.

❹ Turn right at the road junction and walk along the level side lane between fields of grazing cattle and small plots of vegetables. Keep to the right at the next junction, marked by a wayside cross.

❺ Keeping a lookout for speeding traffic, cross the main road and continue ahead along the side lane opposite.

❻ Turn right and follow the country road until it begins to turn sharp left.

❼ Go forwards along the grassy field track, beside sparse woodland, over crosstracks and between open fields.

❽ Turn right then left along a farm track, and go downhill past a farm and out along its drive.

❾ Turn right along the lane, following it above a wooded slope, back to the village. Turn left at the fork, and left again at the D121. Turn right at the end of this road if returning to the château, passing a side street leading to the church along the way.

Points of interest

Ⓐ Viewpoint looking through the ornamental gates into the upper section of the château gardens. Close at hand are the ancient potting sheds and greenhouses where the decorative vegetables and other plants are grown.

Ⓑ Viewpoint looking over the château rooftops towards the Loire.

Ⓒ Trees screen the edge of the Loire's flood plain. The plain dates from the end of the last Ice Age, showing how deeply the river has cut its way into the surrounding soft rock and alluvial soils.

Walk 25
CINQ-MARS-LA-PILE

7 km (4¼ miles)   Easy

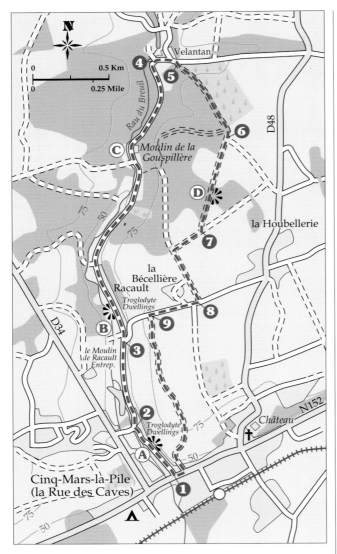

came and established a base there. A massive 30 metre high, ancient tower stands on a cliff above the village; its purpose and its builders are unknown. The tower is known simply as the *'pile'*.

There is an alternative title for the village, which refers to an unusual type of housing there. This is *la Rue des Caves*, a name that describes perfectly the early part of this walk. A low cliff on the eastern side of the valley of a little river, the Breuil, is lined with troglodyte dwellings, some still inhabited. The caves have been simply converted by drilling a hole in the roof to allow smoke to escape and bricking up the entrance with a wall to make a snug home that is cool in summer and dry in winter. Sometimes an existing cave would have been enlarged.

Near the trodlodyte dwellings, pretty flower and vegetable gardens line the roadside, and an old mill higher up the valley has been converted to a *Chambre d'Hôte* which offers bed and breakfast accommodation. Climbing out of the valley, a farm track follows a course between woodland and vineyards towards a modern military installation, before descending into the village.

Cinq-Mars-la-Pile has an ancient château high above the valley road (the N152), to the north-east of the village. Surrounded by a moat, all that remains of the 11th and 12th-century feudal stronghold, are two round towers built around vaulted chambers. The view of the Loire from the roof

With such an intriguing name, Cinq-Mars-la-Pile cries out to be explored. The literal translation is *Fifth of March Electric Battery* or *The tower of the fifth of March,* but no-one seems to know the origin of the name. Standing opposite the River Cher's junction with the Loire, the village was inhabited by Gauls long before the Romans is breathtaking, whilst the gardens are a blend of French formal and English natural style. The château is open every day and guided visits take about 30 minutes. An English language leaflet is available on request.

There are two more châteaux near the village, one on either side of it, which are open to the public. The 13th-century château upstream at Luynes commands a view over the rooftops of 16th-century houses and a massive 15th-century oak-timbered market hall. The château at Langeais, a town famous for melon growing, is approached across a draw-bridge at the top of the narrow main street. Solidly built like a medieval castle, the château was in fact a product of the Renaissance period. It was built by Louis XI as a protection against Breton invaders in the mid-15th century. One of the comfortable apartments contains a waxwork display depicting the marriage of Charles VIII to Anne of Burgundy.

You should study the menus of several of the small restaurants along the main road, or in side streets, when deciding where to lunch. Alternatively, food can be bought locally for a picnic which may be eaten beside the track leading from Velatan, on the return leg of the walk.

How to get there: Cinq-Mars-la-Pile is on the N152 Saumur to Tours road, opposite the junction of the Loire with the River Cher. Park off the main road in the centre of Cinq-Mars-la-Pile.

Route description

1 Follow the signposted Rue des Caves north and away from the main road, along the valley bottom of the River Breuil.

2 Where a side lane turns left, continue along the valley road.

3 Kep going past another road turning right. Go past the troglodyte houses on the village outskirts and along the narrowing wooded valley.

The walk can be shortened by turning right at the *Chambre d'Hôte* sign prior to the bridge. A woodland path climbs steeply to the far side of the forest, and rejoins the described walk on the field track a little to the left of 6.

4 Turn right at the road junction and climb out of the valley bottom.

5 A little uphill and diagonally opposite a road diverging left, turn half right to follow a grassy field track along the woodland edge, past a farm building and to the right of a large area of vineyards. Ignore any narrow tracks into the wood on your right.

6 Bear right at the fork and still beside the wood, walk on towards a large open field. Go past an old barn, then through a wood and out along the boundary between the wood and a field on its far side. Go past a track re-entering the wood to your right.

7 Turn right at the track junction, following it gently downhill to another junction. Turn left at this T-junction and keep to the left along a track to one side of the farm complex at la Bécellière. Turn right on reaching the surfaced lane.

8 Ignore the side turning to the left and begin to go fairly steeply downhill along a surfaced lane.

9 Turn right beside a barn and follow the cart track across fields, then downhill along a gradually improving lane into Cinq-Mars-la-Pile.

Points of interest

A Viewpoint. Without appearing too inquisitive, try to imagine life in the cave houses lining the valley road. Most are converted into garages, and some have modern dwellings built onto them, but one or two are used as holiday cottages. The rooms were carved out of the solid, but easily worked sandstone outcrop lining the valley. Cool in summer and dry in winter, they made extremely comfortable homes.

B Viewpoint. Look over the wall on the left. The well-tended riverside cottage gardens make excellent photographs.

C The attractive old water mill of la Gouspillère has been converted into a comfortable *Chambre d'Hôte*.

D Viewpoint. The radar towers are part of the French military's Early Warning System. Beyond them stretches the more peaceful view of the Loire and Cher valleys.

Walk 26
ETANG DE MARSON
4 km (2½ miles)   Easy

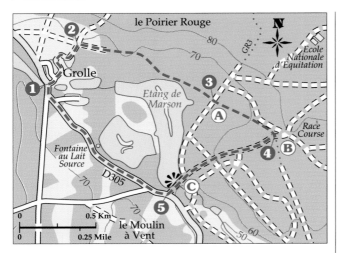

Race-horses have been trained in the Saumur district for centuries, and the city is also the home of French Cavalry regiments. It is not surprising, therefore, to find the National Equestrian School in a forest close to the city boundary.

This walk takes a route through forest surrounding an attractive reservoir, south of Saumur. The walk starts at the secluded village of Grolle on the D161, a minor road winding through ancient forest. You will cross asparagus fields to reach woodland screening the riding school. The return is via the shore of a small reservoir, the Etang de Marson.

The name Saumur literally means 'safe wall'. The city lies beneath the protection of its white-walled castle, which is topped by a pepperpot tower and stands high up on a rocky outcrop. Saumur fits between the rivers Loire and Thouet, where fishermen have been employed since the reign of 'Good King René' in the 15th century. There are several museums in and around the old town; the Museum of Decorative Arts, the Horse Museum and the Cavalry School Museum are the best. There is even a museum devoted to the craft of mushroom farming, which makes use of the man-made caves in the chalk cliffs. In addition, several wine merchants invite visitors to sample the local vintages; the sparkling wines from Hilaire St. Florent are particularly interesting. Weekly open-air markets are held along the old quayside.

Saumur has a wide range of restaurants.

How to get there: Take the N147 south from Saumur, then turn right along the D960 to a crossroads by the Château de Presle. Turn right onto the D305 and follow it through Marson, past the tree-shaded reservoir on your right, into Grolle. Park beneath trees at the roadside, on the outskirts of the village.

Route description

❶ Leave the main road and walk through Grolle and through scattered woodland on its far side, then out along a track leading towards asparagus fields.

❷ Turn right at the track junction and go slightly downhill from the fields and into the pine forest. Follow the woodland path gradually down towards the lake, then above its shore.

❸ Cross a wider track and go gently uphill, still in forest, to reach the boundary fence of the National Riding School.

❹ Turn right, away from the boundary fence of the race course, then walk downhill. Go over crosstracks and bear left on joining a track crossing the reservoir dam.

❺ Turn right at the road and follow it back towards Grolle.

Points of interest

Ⓐ A track crossing the path is part of the GR3, the long distance pathway following a 275 km (170 mile) route along the Loire Valley.

Ⓑ The *École Nationale d'Equitation* is France's premier riding school. From this vantage point, you can see young race-horses and trainee jockeys being put through their paces. The complex of buildings glimpsed at the end of the ride is the school's stables and indoor training blocks.

Ⓒ Viewpoint. Trees frame a pretty view of the reedy shores and waters of the Etang de Marson.

Walk 27
CHANZEAUX

6 km (3¾ miles)   Easy/Moderate

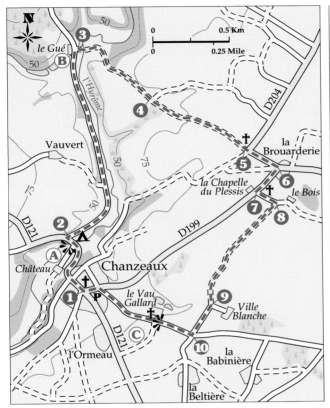

Route description

❶ Follow the main road (the D121) downhill from the church and across the river.

❷ Turn right away from the main road and follow the tree-lined side lane downstream, along the riverside.

❸ Where the road begins to swing left uphill, turn sharp right and go through a gate. Follow a field track, going over the river then uphill along a grassy track climbing above a narrow dry valley.

❹ Go forwards at the track junction, across the head of another small wooded side valley and follow the now sunken track between fields.

❺ Walk forwards from the way-side cross when the track joins a road. Follow the road into the farming hamlet of la Brouarderie.

❻ Turn right at the junction and walk on to the next building.

❼ Turn left beside a cross opposite the farm, and follow the side lane signposted to le Bois.

❽ Do not go as far as the farmhouse, but turn right along a grassy field track.

❾ Go forwards by a farm drive, and walk down to the side road.

❿ Turn right at the crossroads and follow the lane downhill, past a shrine marking the entrance to a large farm, and back to Chanzeaux.

Points of interest

Ⓐ Viewpoint. The privately owned château sits above tranquil meadows lining the water-lily filled River Hyrôme.

Ⓑ The name of the farm on the left, le Gué, indicates that there was once a ford across the river at this point.

Ⓒ Viewpoint. A small roadside cross makes an ideal foreground for a view overlooking Chanzeaux.

Chanzeaux is almost unknown outside the region, but the few visitors who turn off the N160 discover a sunny rural village linked to a romantic château. Chanzeaux faces south-west on gently sloping ground above the River Hyrôme, a northward flowing tributary of the Layon.

The walk starts in the village, then follows a meandering tree-lined stream before climbing up to meadows and small woods. Quiet lanes and ancient field tracks make this a simple walk to follow as well as being a pleasant ramble in little visited countryside.

There is a small but well-appointed riverside campsite downstream of the château.

Chanzeaux has a good selection of family-run bars/restaurants and enough shops to provide the essentials for a good picnic.

How to get there: Chanzeaux is at the junction of the D199 and D121 roads, south-east along the D121 from the N160 Angers to Chemillé road. The car park is 50 metres from the church along the D199 le Champ-sur-Layon road.

Walk 28
DOLMEN DE LA MADELEINE   7 km (4¼ miles)   Easy/Moderate

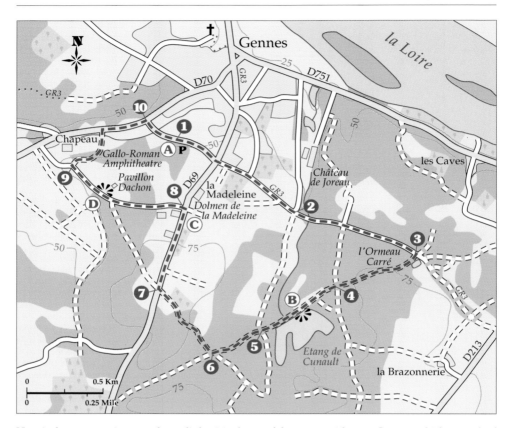

Here is the opportunity to explore a little visited part of the countryside near Gennes, which is south of the Loire between Saumur and Angers. Using quiet back lanes and field tracks, the walk starts beside a recently discovered small Gallo-Roman amphitheatre a little to the south of the town. The walk then follows part of the GR3 Loire Valley long distance footpath into wooded countryside, then returns to Gennes. On the way back, the route passes the highlight of this walk, a massive dolmen – a stone structure built over 4500 years ago for an unknown purpose.

Gennes is a pleasant little town built above an ancient river crossing over the Loire. There has been a town on the site since pre-Roman times. A rather fine château, the Château de Joreau sits below a steeply wooded slope to the east of the town. It is privately owned and is only open to the public for special events.

Refreshments can be obtained in Gennes, or from the supermarket passed on the early part of the walk, between ❶ and ❷.

How to get there: Gennes is on the D751 Loire Valley road between Saumur and Angers. From Gennes, follow either the D70 Louerre road or the D69 Doué-la-Fontaine road southwards for just half a kilometre (a little over a quarter of a mile), then turn down the link road between the D69 and D70, which will be signposted to the Gallo-Roman amphitheatre. Park in the layby next to the excavation site.

Route description

1 Walk uphill along the road from the amphitheatre site. Cross the main road at the traffic island and follow the lane opposite, passing the supermarket complex on your left before moving out into open country and joining a side lane from your left.

2 Go over a minor crossroads then walk ahead, downhill then up, into natural woodland. Continue beyond the next crossroads and ignore minor woodland tracks to the left and right.

3 Where the lane makes a small but sharp double bend a little way beyond the 9-ton weight limit and 50 kph signs, turn right along a forest track. Follow yellow blobs and white/red striped waymarks past a small pond and into woodland.

4 Still following the waymarks, go over crosstracks and walk downhill to a reservoir. Continue along the forest track and across the dam.

5 Leaving the white/red waymarks, go forwards at a slightly staggered crosstracks, gently uphill through the forest.

6 Turn right at the crossing, still walking uphill beside a clearing, then go into natural woodland for the last time before you pass a plantation.

7 Turn right on reaching the main road and walk along the left-hand side of it, facing oncoming traffic. Go past a small industrial site on your left, then downhill to a minor crossroads. The short track leading to the dolmen is on the right.

8 Walk back to the main road from the dolmen, and cross over it. Walk gently downhill along the side lane opposite, beneath the shady branches of mostly deciduous natural woodland.

9 Where the lane starts to swing left, turn sharp right and walk steeply downhill, through a narrow wood, then to the right of a building materials factory in order to reach the road. Turn right and walk to the road junction on the outskirts of Gennes.

10 Turn right at the road junction. The amphitheatre layby is a little way uphill on the right.

Points of interest

A The Amphitheatre. The Loire was the boundary between the Roman provinces of *Lugdunensis* to the north and *Aquitania*. Gennes guarded the river crossing of a minor north-south road. Fragments of an aqueduct and a temple have been found, but most of the recent archaeological work is concentrated on the small Gallo-Roman amphitheatre. As the site is run mostly by volunteers, the rather complex opening times when there will be a specialist on site are:
April to June – Saturdays 15.00-17.00;
July/August – Daily 10.00-12.00 & 14.30-18.30;
September – Sundays 15.00-16.00 or at 18.00.
At all other times it is possible to get a good impression of the site simply by looking over the wire fence separating it from the nearby field, beyond the layby.

B Viewpoint overlooking the reedy tree-lined Etang de Cunault, where birdlife is abundant in the semi-natural environment.

C The dolmen is thought to have been built in the Middle Neolithic period, about 2500 BC. Underneath the massive top stone are what appear to be the remains of a comparatively modern bread oven.

D Viewpoint. The ruined tower, the Pavillon Dachon, was a hunting tower. From there, the ladies from the nearby Château de Joreau watched the chase in the days before Gennes and its surrounding farmland began to encroach on the game forest.

Walk 29
LE PORT DE VALLEE

6 km (3¾ miles)   Easy

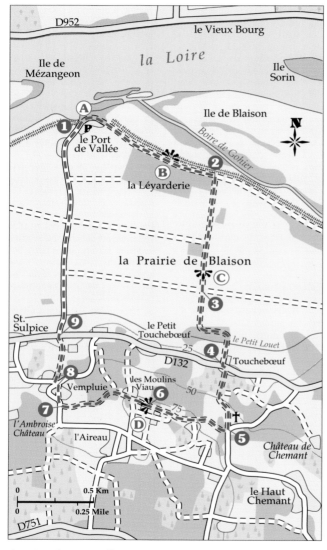

upstream from Angers. The levels were ignored until the 20th century except to exploit their high grade alluvial soil. Beyond them, a short, steep climb leads through a series of pretty hamlets. You will pass the boundary wall of a minor château on the way back, before descending steeply to the flood plain again, where an almost arrow-straight lane leads directly towards the beckoning restaurant.

If you cannot summon the energy to do the walk, a shorter version of this route can be followed by horse and carriage! A friendly horse, based at the riverside restaurant, will pull a small carriage around the tracks enclosing the Prairie de Blaison.

Angers, across the river from Le Port de Vallée, is the principal city of the Loire. Its old quarter is bordered by tree-lined boulevards, making it a pleasant place to visit on a hot day. A blue-grey roofed château with 17 towers stands above the city. It was built in the 15th century on the site of a third century fortress. Until Joan of Arc helped to drive the English out of France, Angers marked the border between English held lands and those of the French. Tapestries are an important aspect of the internal decoration of the château; of the many on display, *la Dame à l'Orgue* in the Logis Royal, and the *Apocalypse* in the Logis du Gouverneur, are worth a special mention. The latter is 100 metres long and 5 metres high, depicting on a red velvet background the tortures of the

A major advantage offered by this walk is that it starts and finishes at a restaurant. What better motivation than to know that a meal in pleasant surroundings awaits you?

Starting at the old ferry station of le Port de Vallée, the walk follows a series of tracks across the ancient flood plain of the Loire, damned. Despite its great proportions, the surviving tapestry is only two thirds of its original length. *La Dame à l'Orgue* is Flemish; as the title suggests, it portrays a woman playing the organ.

Tapestries elsewhere are also significant among the art treasures of Angers. The Ancien Hôpital de St. John has a permanent exhibition of modern work by Jean Lurçat. Addressing 20th-century themes, it includes *The Man of Hiroshima* and *The End of Everything*. Abusson tapestries hang in the cathderal, beside beautiful stained glass dating from the 12th century.

Half-timbered houses, many at least six storeys high, line the side streets and market squares of Angers, and tucked away to the west of the Logis Barrault is a garden where the ruins of an arsenal, accidentally blown up in 1815, are now a haven of tranquillity.

Whilst it is possible to find an alternative restaurant in nearby St. Sulpice, the walk is planned around the one by the riverside at le Port de Vallée. Anyone carrying a picnic on the walk should aim to have it beneath the shade of trees in the little wood to the west of the hamlet of les Moulins Viau, which is between **6** and **7**, a bit more than half-way round .

How to get there: Take the D751 Gennes road south-west from Angers. Turn left at St. Jean des Mauvrets onto the D132, the old valley road. Drive through St. Sulpice and take the first road on the left beyond the village. Follow this part-surfaced side lane all the way to the river bank at le Port de Vallée. Park near the restaurant.

Route description

1 Follow the unsurfaced track upstream along the embankment, away from the restaurant and through woodland bordering the Ile de Blaison.

2 Turn right at the edge of the wood to follow a side track heading towards higher ground in the distance.

3 Go over the crosstracks, continue in a straight line, then on entering a small wood, turn left and then right to leave the wood. Walk towards a group of small houses next to the road at the foot of the wooded escarpment ahead.

4 Cross the road and climb the narrow sunken track opposite, past small vineyards and then scrub woodland at a higher level.

5 On reaching a side lane, turn right at a wayside cross, and walk along a level track across the hillside, passing scattered buildings.

6 Go past a couple of farms, keeping ahead and ignoring two tracks to the right and one to the left. Walk on towards a wood, then on entering, take the left-hand track at a fork. Cross the terraced hillside above a small hamlet.

7 At the road, turn right, downhill, then almost immediately take a narrow lane on the right, through the hamlet of Vempluie.

8 When you rejoin the road, cross the T-junction by going diagonally left. Follow the side lane opposite for about 30 metres, then turn right and walk down a steep sunken track to reach the main road.

9 Cross the main road and walk down the straight part-surfaced lane in order to reach le Port de Vallée.

Points of interest

Ⓐ Le Port de Vallée. A ferry once crossed the river at this point and commercial craft loaded and unloaded cargo here, hence the word 'port' in the title. Punts moored below the restaurant are used by fishermen on this shallow section of the river.

Ⓑ Viewpoint. The land to the east of Le Port de Vallée is an island, the Ile de Blaison, which has been created by an oxbow loop of the Loire, the reed-lined Boire de Gohier.

Ⓒ Viewpoint. Tiny hamlets line the escarpment, marking the limit of the Loire's ancient flood plain. The river deposited millions of tonnes of fine alluvial soil, which is now excellent agricultural land.

Ⓓ Viewpoint. Many of the interesting hamlets passed along the track have been here for centuries. Ahead and beyond the small forest is the attractive privately-owned château of Ambroise.

Walk 30
BEAULIEU-SUR-LAYON

8.5 km (5¼ miles) or 5 km (3 miles)
Strenuous with one steep 60m (197ft) climb;
Moderate alternative

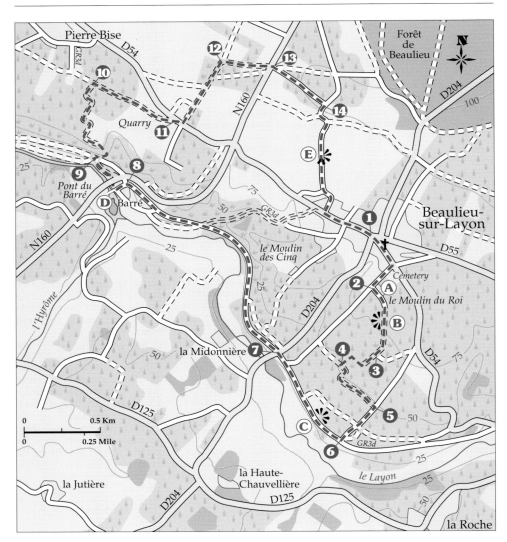

The predominantly flat land south of the Loire is cut by the steep valley of the River Layon. This walk begins in the wine-growing village of Beaulieu-sur-Layon and passes through the vineyards on its south-facing slopes, where the famous Anjou vintages grow. An easy track follows the line of an abandoned railway beside the River Layon, but after it crosses the N160, the terrain is harder going until you reach the top of an old limestone quarry. The return route is through upland vineyards and open fields to recross the N160. Country lanes will then take you downhill, back into the centre of Beaulieu.

If you would prefer not to tackle the steep climb, the walk can be shortened by following a side path up the dry narrow valley prior to reaching the N160.

A small museum in Beaulieu-sur-Layon, the Cadeau de Vin, is devoted to the history of Anjou wine growing, including an exhibition of old bottles and glasses. The museum is signposted from the village, and is open every day throughout the year.

There are several restaurants in Beaulieu and one at the Pont du Barré, which marks the half-way point. The riverside next to the bridge is ideal for an informal picnic or, if this area is crowded, you can sit down under the trees beyond ❾.

How to get there: Take the N160 Angers to Chemillé road towards the Layon Valley, then go east along the D54, signposted to Beaulieu-sur-Layon. Park in the village centre, near the church.

Route description

❶ From the church walk down the D54 Rablay-sur-Layon road for 250 metres, then turn right to go downhill along a narrow side lane, the Rue Moulin du Roy.

❷ Turn left along another side lane and go past the stump of an old windmill, then downhill towards a series of vineyards.

❸ Where a side track leaves to your left, continue ahead and downhill. Swing right then left with a footpath, around a small wooded area surrounded by vineyards.

❹ At a track junction, go left then right, then left again, zig-zagging downhill between the vines before reaching a level section of the track which leads towards a narrow lane.

❺ Turn right when you reach the lane, and go downhill, past a couple of farms and towards the valley floor.

❻ Turn right and follow the lane between flowering hedges and mature trees, within sight of the river.

❼ Cross the D204 linking Beaulieu with villages to the south, and continue to walk along the valley floor, with a steep scrub-covered slope on your right and meadows beside the river on your left.

The walk can be shortened by turning right after about 2 km (just over a mile), to follow a narrow track uphill along the scrubby dry valley. You will emerge on the western outskirts of Beaulieu. (If visiting the restaurant at the Pont du Barré, continue down the main valley, then return to the turn-off afterwards.)

❽ Do not go as far as the busy N160, but avoid it by turning left next to the restaurant and going down to the river. Turn right and go under the road bridge. Follow the path to the right, back to the lane along the valley bottom.

❾ Immediately cross the lane and enter overgrown old quarry workings. Following occasional white/red waymarks on rocks, go to the right below boulders and beneath the abandoned quarry, and follow a stony path uphill to a prominent limestone spur. Climb down, bearing left from the top of the spur, into a small area of scrub, then climb up the narrow zig-zagging path to easier ground, where an improving track leads through vineyards sheltered from the wind by lines of cypress trees.

❿ Leaving the waymarked track, turn right at the junction and follow a track going downhill above the rim of a modern limestone quarry.

⓫ Turn right on joining the road, then after roughly 100 metres, turn left along a tree-shaded farm track, going gently uphill between fields. Keep ahead at the next three track junctions then go over a slight rise covered by vines and scrub.

⓬ Turn right at the crossing. Walk on between vineyards until you reach the main road.

⓭ Take great care crossing the busy N160 – it can seem like a race track at times! Go diagonally right onto a minor side road signposted to Beaulieu-sur-Layon. Go past a farmhouse and beside vineyards.

⓮ Follow the road as it turns right, then left past the drive to a large farm, and right again, through three right-angled bends. Continue downhill along the tree-lined by-road, between open fields and into the western outskirts of Beaulieu. When you reach the D54, turn left to return to the church in the centre of the village.

Points of interest

Ⓐ The stone tower on your left, its sails long gone, is all that remains of a windmill, the Moulin du Roi. The name-plate for the street leading to the mill uses the old spelling 'roy' for 'king', but the French IGN map-makers use the modern 'roi'. The king in question was 'Good King René', who ruled over this part of France in the 15th century.

Ⓑ Viewpoint. Grapes for the Anjou vintages grow on the south-facing slopes above the Layon Valley.

Ⓒ Viewpoint. Hang gliders can often be seen soaring on updraughts high above the tranquil River Layon.

Ⓓ The old bridge, the shady Pont du Barré, was in past times used by pack-horses and farm carts. It is now an ideal resting place.

Ⓔ Viewpoint looking over Beaulieu-sur-Layon.

BARTHOLOMEW WALK GUIDES

Bartholomew publishes an extensive range of Walk Guides covering some of the best walking country in Britain and France.

Titles in the series include:

Walking in Brittany
Walking in the Dordogne
Walking in Provençe

Walk the Cornish Coastal Path
Walk the Cotswolds
Walk the Dales
Walk Dorset & Thomas Hardy's Wessex
Walk Kent
Walk the Lakes
More Walks in the Lakes
Walk Loch Lomond & the Trossachs
Walk Loch Ness & the Spey Valley
Walk the New Forest
Walk the North York Moors
Walk Northumbria
Walk Oban, Mull & Lochaber
Walk the Peak District
Walk Perthshire
Walk Skye & Wester Ross
Walk Snowdonia & North Wales
Walk South Devon Coastal Path & Dartmoor

All titles are available from good bookshops,
or telephone HarperCollins Distribution Services
on 0141-772 3200.